South Carolina Marriages

1800-1820

South Carolina Marriages

1800-1820

Compiled by

BRENT H. HOLCOMB

INTRODUCTION

HIS SECOND VOLUME of South Carolina marriages, like the first—which covered the years from 1688 to 1799—has been compiled from a variety of sources, exclusive of newspapers. The sources of the marriage records are identified in abbreviated form at the end of each entry. These abbreviated references are listed and explained below. Some sources used in the first volume continued into the period of this volume, though most did not extend that far. Some later marriage records have been located which cover a larger geographical area than was the case with the first volume.

Of prime importance in this volume are marriage records (especially marriage settlements) from "burnt districts," mainly Beaufort, Colleton, and Georgetown. Within these marriage settlements are important references to deceased parents, grandparents, or other deceased relatives of one of the contracting parties, and to former husbands of the brides. These records are clues to approximate death dates which may not be available elsewhere. In the case of marriage settlements, the entire document should be read for names that are vital to a particular search. The abstracts included here are necessarily brief: some marriage settlements run ten pages or more, and references to wills or estates might be found within the body of the document.

This volume does not include marriage notices from newspapers. Most of these have already been published, including the following which I have compiled: *Marriage and Death Notices from The (Charleston) Times, 1800-1821; Marriage, Death, and Estate Notices from Georgetown, S. C. Newspapers, 1791-1861; Marriage and Death Notices from Camden, S. C. Newspapers, 1816-1861;* and *Marriage and Death Notices from the Pendleton (S.C.) Messenger, 1807-1851.*

I am indebted to the following persons for supplying records: Mr. W. E. Howell of Sumter, South Carolina for the references from the John Blount Miller diary; Mr. G. Howard Bryan of Jacksonville, Florida and Miss Nettie Wheeler of Farmersville, Alabama for the entries from the Bryan journal; and the Rev. Fr. Charles Rowland for entries from St. Mary's Roman Catholic Church register.

BRENT H. HOLCOMB, C.A.L.S.
Columbia, South Carolina

SOURCES

Bryan Journal	Journal of Richard Bryan, a Methodist minister and justice of the peace in Colleton District. Original in possession of Miss Nettie Wheeler, Farmersville, Alabama.
Bush R MM	Bush River Monthly Meeting Minutes. Original in the Quaker Collection, Guilford College, N. C. Published in Hinshaw's *Encyclopedia of American Quaker Genealogy.*
Cane Cr MM	Cane Creek Monthly Meeting Minutes. Original in the Quaker Collection, Guilford College, N. C. Published in Hinshaw's *Encyclopedia of American Quaker Genealogy.*
Chaston ML	Charleston District Marriage Licenses as found in the Ordinary's Journal. Originals in South Carolina Archives. Published in *The South Carolina Magazine of Ancestral Research.*
Chaston Pro J	Charleston District Marriage Licenses as found in the Ordinary's Journal. Originals in the office of the Probate Judge, Charleston County Court House.
Darl MB	Darlington District Marriage Bonds. Originals in the Darlington County Court House. Published in *The South Carolina Magazine of Ancestral Research.*
Drehr Journal	Journal of the Rev. Godfrey Drehr, 1819-1851. Microfilm copy at the South Caroliniana Library, Columbia, S. C. Published by Southern Historical Press.
Georgetown Meth Ch	Records of Georgetown Methodist Church. Published in *The South Carolina Historical and Genealogical Magazine (SCH&G).*
Holy Cross Ch	Records of Holy Cross (Episcopal) Church, Stateburg, S. C. Originals in the South Carolina Historical Society, Charleston.

Horry DB	Horry County Deed Book, followed by volume and page number. Original in the Horry County Court House, Conway, S. C.
John Blount Miller Diary	In the Sumter County Historical Society Archives, Sumter, S. C.
Kershaw Diary	Diary of James Kershaw. Original at the South Caroliniana Library, Columbia, S. C. Some entries published in *Historic Camden*, by Kirkland and Kennedy.
Mar Set	Marriage Settlements, a series at South Carolina Archives; followed by volume and page number.
Marion ML	Marion District Marriage Licenses. Originals in Marion County Court House, Marion, S. C. Published in *SCH&G*.
Marlboro ML	Marlboro District Marriage Licenses. Originals within volumes of probate records in Marlboro County Court House, Bennettsville, S. C. Published in *National Genealogical Society Quarterly*.
Marlboro Pro Journal	Marriage licenses found within probate journal.
Misc Rec	Miscellaneous Records, a series at South Carolina Archives; followed by volume and page number.
Moses Waddel	List of marriages performed by Rev. Moses Waddel. Published as a separate volume.
Newberry Will Book C	Original in Newberry County Court House, Newberry, S. C.
Pen DB	Pendleton (Anderson) District Deed Book, followed by volume and page number. Original at South Carolina Archives.
Piney Grove MM	Piney Grove Monthly Meeting Minutes. Original in the Quaker Collection, Guilford College, N. C. Published in Hinshaw's *Encyclopedia of American Quaker Genealogy*.
Pr Geo Winyaw	Records of Prince George's Winyaw (Episcopal) Church. Typescript in the South Carolina Historical Society, Charleston.

St Hel PR	St. Helena Parish Register. Published in *SCH&G*.
St Mary's RC	Records of St. Mary's Roman Catholic Church, Charleston, S. C. Originals at the church.
St Matthews Luth Ch	Records of St. Matthews Lutheran Church, St. Matthews, S. C. Originals at the South Caroliniana Library, Columbia, S. C. Published in *The South Carolina Magazine of Ancestral Research*.
St Michaels Luth Ch	Irmo, S. C. Published in *The South Carolina* Records of St. Michael's Lutheran Church, *Magazine of Ancestral Research*.
St Phil PR	St. Philip's Parish Register, Charleston, S. C. Published as separate volumes.
Wmbg DB	Williamsburg County Deed Books, followed by volume and page number. Originals in Williamsburg County Court House, Kingstree, S. C.
York Pro	York Probate Records, followed by estate package number. Originals in York County Court House, York, S. C. Published in *National Genealogical Society Quarterly*.
2d Pres Ch	List of marriages from the Second Presbyterian Church, Charleston, S. C. Typescript in Richland County Library, Columbia, S. C.

SOUTH CAROLINA MARRIAGES 1800-1820

Aaron, slave of Mrs. Washington, & Daphne, free woman of color, 7 Jan 1819. St Phil PR

Abbergotte, Joseph of St. Helena Parish, Beaufort Dist., and Mary E. Featherstone, 14 Nov 1820; David Turner, trustee; William Russell, John Perryclear, John Scanlan, wit. Mar Set 8: 120-121

Abbott, Mr. & Miss Lucy Breed, 4 May 1810. Kershaw Diary

Aberegg, John of Charleston, watchmaker, & Julie Vigier, of same, widow, 17 March 1814; John Jacob Schnell, grocer, trustee; Lewis Roux, Peter Artman, Pr. Rigaud, wit. Mar Set 6: 314-318

Abraham, slave of Mr. Ed Simons & Celia, slave of Mr. K. G. Simons, 16 July 1818 in Charleston. St Phil PR

Abram, slave of Miss M. Deas, & Molly, slave of Mrs. L. Hutchinson, 21 Oct 1820 in Charleston. St Phil PR

Ackis, John, of Charleston, shoemaker, and Charlotte Hogarth, of the same place, spinster, 19 Aug 1802. St Phil PR

Adams, David L. & Mary B. Milligan, 3 Dec 1811. 2d Pres Ch

Adams, Godfrey of Abbeville District, & Jane Hoff of St. Bartholomews Parish, widow, 6 April 1805; Richard Singellton, of said parish, planter, trustee; Jacob S. V. M. Hoff, Thos Stevens, wit. Mar Set 5: 79-84

Adams, Jonathan, & Mary Bright, to Rev. Robert Purnell, 4 March 1816. Marlboro ML

Adams, W. M. & Julah Bullard, of Marlboro, to Rev. Wm. Bennett, 18 Aug 1813. Marlboro ML

Adamson, Wm. & Amelia Alexander, 23 Sept 1800. Kershaw Diary

1

Addison, James & Mrs. Eliza Fordham, 30 May 1818 in St.
Thomas Parish. St Phil PR

Addison, Joseph of St. Thomas, planter, & Sophia Taylor,
of Charleston, widow, to Rev. William Percy, 25 Jan
1809. Chaston ML

Aiken, William of Charleston, merchant, & Henrietta Wyat,
of the same place, spinster, 11 Nov 1801. St. Phil PR

Air, James Henry (Dr.), & Harriott Atkinson, 2 Feb 1802;
Isaac Holmes, Solomon Legare, esqrs., trustees; William A. Moultrie, wit. Mar Set 4: 141-145

Aitchison, Wm of Charleston & Mary Murray, of Charleston,
spinster, 18 Oct 1811; William Russell, Thomas Denny,
trustees; James Dennison, Jas Nicholson, wit. Mar
Set 6: 72-78

Albert, slave of Miss Wakefield & Jemima, slave of Mrs.
Anne Thompson, 4 June 1818 in Charleston. St. Phil PR

Aldrich, Robert & Ann Hawkins Libby, 4 June 1811; William Libby, Robert Little, trustees; John R. Wyatt, N.
Hawes, wit. Mar Set 6: 61-63

Alexander, John H. of Colleton Dist., & Jane North of
same, 27 May 1809; Hans McCullough, William McCullough, wit. Mar Set 5: 477-478

Alexander, William, of Charleston, & Mary Witter, 28 Jan
1801; William Bee & Jacob Axson, trustees; Saml E. Axson, Jane Holmes, Ann Axson, wit. Mar Set 4: 25-28

Allan, William of Charleston, merchant, & Sarah Haig,
spinster, 17 April 1801; Robert McKewn Haig, Charles
Elliott Rowand, trustees; Elizabeth L. Hutchinson,
Jane S. Blake, wit. Mar Set 4: 92-95

Allen, Benj. & Mary Green, 8 Aug 1816. Bryan Journal

Allen, William & Margaret Jones, 1 Jan 1805. Moses
Waddel

Allison, Francis & Mary Ann Greaves, 12 Nov 1805; license
directed to Revd. Thomas Humphries. Marion ML

Allston, Benjamin the elder, of Waccamaw, & Mary Coachman of Charleston, 16 Dec 1808; James William Gadsden
of Charleston, trustee; Benjamin Singellton, Jas.
Nicholson, wit. Mar Set 5: 420-427

Allston, Benjamin Senr. of Waccamaw, planter, & Mary Coachman, of Charleston, spinster, to Rev. James D. Simons, 15 Dec 1808. Chaston ML

Allston, Joseph W. & Sarah Prior, 15 Dec 1818, at Georg-
town.   Pr Geo Winyaw

Allston, Josias & Anna Maria Taylor, daughter of Mary
Taylor, decd., all of George Town, 12 June 1802; John
Cassels, Savage Smith, trustees; Mary Godfrey, wit.
Mar Set 4: 192-198

Allston, Josias of Georgetown, Esquire, & Anna Maria Tay-
lor, spinster (already married), 28 Dec 1804; John
Cassels, Savage Smith, trustees; John Taylor Jr., wit.
Mar Set 5: 45-50

Ally, slave of Pender (a colored free person) & Myra,
slave of P. Gadsden family, 30 Dec 1814 in Charleston.
St. Phil PR

Alston, William of Georgetown, physician, & Mary Pyatt,
daughter of the late John Pyatt, Esqr. decd & his wife
Elizabeth, sister of Thomas Labruce; John Labruce &
Benjamin Allston Sr., Esqr., trustees; Rd. Brownfield,
Danl DuPre, Josias Allston, wit., 1 Feb 1800.   Mar
Set 3, pp. 429-434

Amos, slave of Col. Danl. Srevens, & Roseanna, slave
Estate Benj. Cudworth, 22 Dec 1814 in Charleston.   St
Phil PR

Ancrum, James Hasell of Charleston, & Jane Washington,
daughter of the Hon. William Washington & Jane Riely
his wife, daughter of Charles Elliott, late of St.
Paul's Parish, 10 Nov 1801; James Reid Pringle, Josiah
Taylor, wit.   Mar Set 4: 150-153

Ancrum, Wm. Jr. & Miss Brisbane, 26 July 1802.   Kershaw
Diary

Anderson, _____ B. & Eliza Denison, before 1810, by
Samuel Leard.   Georgetown Meth Ch

Anderson, James & Mary Hamlin, spinster of Christ Church
Parish, 3 May 1820; Thomas Hamlin, Jno Hamlin, trustees; Susan Hamlin, John Whitesides, wit.   Mar Set 8:
150-153

Anderson, John-Southgate, of Charleston, mariner & Issa-
bella Grierson of Charleston, widow, 1 July 1808, to
Rev. George Buist.   Chaston ML

Anderson, William & Hannah Smith, 8 Jan 1814, in Charleston.   St Phil PR

Anderson, William Wallace M. D. & Mary Jane Mackenzie, daughter of John Mackenzie and Elizabeth Heron his wife, granddaughter of Captain Benjamin Heron, 30 Jan 1818. Holy Cross Ch

Andrews, Moses & Louisa Blackley, 31 March 1814, in Charleston. St Phil PR

Angel, Justus of Charleston, gentleman, & Martha Waight, daughter of the late Isaac Waight, Esqr., 23 Nov 1810; Major John Jenkins of St. Helena, John P. Wilhelmi, trustees; Robert Cohen, Robert Tennant, wit. Mar Set 6: 2-4

Angel, Justus of Charleston, Merchant, & Martha Waight, of St. Helena, spinster, to Rev. John Buchan, 23 Nov 1810. Chaston ML

Ansley, Andrew & Sarah Lowry, 30 Sept 1806. Moses Waddel

Ansley, Thomas & Mary McKinley, 13 Oct 1807. Moses Waddel

Anthony, S. C. Capt. & Jane Brown, 23 Nov 1813. 2d Pres Ch

Antoine, John & Mrs. Margaret Daly, 20 Feb 1819 in Charleston. St Phil PR

Antony, Micajah T. & Mary R. Dubose, 16 April 1817. Moses Waddel

Archy, slave of Mr. Wm Dewees & Violetta, slave of Estate of Wm Moer, 21 April 1816 in Charleston. St Phil PR

Ardis, Abram & Sarah Bender, widow, both of Edgefield Dist., 24 Apr 1809; Cradk. Burwell, John Clarke, wit. Misc Rec B, pp. 594-595

Ardis, John & Miss Mary Whipple, 18 Dec 1818 in Charleston. St Phil PR

Armenet, Pierre & Marie Paradis, 16 April 1810. St. Mary's RC

Armstrong, Archibald & Miss Susan Duval, 24 Nov 1819 in Charleston. St Phil PR

Arthur, Joseph R. of Charleston, & Mary Y. Simons, 20 Jan 1819; James E. B. Finley, Mary Finley, wit. Mar Set 7: 333-334

Ash, Samuel of Charleston, & Mary Elizabeth Pinckney,
minor daughter of Hopson Pinckney, and wife Mary, late
of St. Thomas Parish, decd., 24 Nov 1812; George Paddon Bond Hasell, physician, Andrew Hasell, William
Johnston, trustees; Thos Doughty, Paul Weston, wit.
Mar Set 6: 157-162

Ashe, Charles C. of Barnwell Dist., & Mary Margaret Gough
of St. Bartholomew's Parish, spinster, 19 April 1810;
George William Gough, trustee; Richard Singellton,
W. Youngblood, Wm. Fishburne Jun., wit.   Mar Set 5:
544-547

Aspray, John Faledo, & Jane Nelson, widow, 9 Dec 1800.
St Phil PR

Axon, John & Miss Mary Gibbes, 2 Dec 1819 in Charleston.
St Phil PR

Axson, John of St. John's Parish, & Ann Jones of same
widow, 1 Dec 1802; Robert McKelvey, Peter Oliver,
Henry Purkey, trustees; Samuel Axson, Robert Wm Rogers,
Wm. Owens, wit.   Mar Set 4: 238-240

Axton, John & Magdelen Huber, 5 March 1801. St. Matthews
Luth Ch

Bacon, Edmund Parks & Martha Weed, 30 June 1812.   Moses
Waddel

Bacot, Peter, & Hannah Mason, license dated 30 May 1804;
married by James Coleman, 6 June 1804.   Darl MB

Bacot, Thomas W. Jr. & Miss Harriet S. Wainwright, 14
March 1816 in Charleston. St. Phil PR

Badger, James Jun. & Mary Blaylock Bell, 26 Feb 1815. 2d
Pres Ch

Bailey, James & Rebeckah Evans, 29 Aug 1816.   Bryan
Journal

Baker, Alpheus, of Abbeville Dist., S. C., & Eliza H.
Courtney, of Wilkes Col, Ga., 9 Apr 1820; F. B. T.
Brown, Harriet P. Baker, wit.   Misc Rec. D, pp. 208-
209

Baker, John J. & Susanna Kennedy, marriage to occur 14
Oct 1802; Henry Duffy, Thomas Denny, wit.   Mar Set
4: 237-238

Baker, John Jonathan, of Charleston, plaisterer, & Susanna Kennedy, of the same place, widow, 14 Oct 1802.
St Phil PR

Baldaree, Sterling & Ruth Waters, both of Newberry Dist.,
6 Feb 1819; B. H. Gray, Rauman Snellgrove, wit.   Misc
Rec D, pp. 135-136

Baldwin, Charles, son of Daniel & Mary Baldwin, Guilford
Co., N. C., & Sarah Thomas, daughter of John & Molley
Thomas, Marlborough Dist., S. C., 25 Dec 1806. Piney
Grove MM

Baldwin, Daniel, son of Daniel & Mary Baldwin, Guilford
Co., N. C., & Christian Wilcuts, daughter of Thomas
& Milly Wilcuts, Marlborough Dist., S. C., 21 May 1812.
Piney Grove MM

Baldwin, Robert, a free blackman, house carpenter & Flora
Garden, a free mustee, 5 Sept 1801; John Rose, trustee;
Mary J. Deady, wit.   Mar Set 4: 128-129

Ball, Archibald of Charleston, & Mary St. Johns, young-
est daughter of James St. Johns of Johns Island, 20
Feb 1800; Lambert Lance & John Marshall Jr., trustees;
Mary Ann Jefferys, Ann Elizabeth Wilkie, Lambert Gough
Lance, wit.   Mar Set 3, pp. 421-425

Ball, Archibald S. & Elizabeth St. John Ball of John's
Island, widow, 7 Sept 1813; William B. Tucker, Charles
S. Tucker, trustees; Saml Parker, Sebastian Keeley,
wit.   Mar Set 6: 263-267

Ball, Archibald Scott & Mary Gough, spinster, 20 Feb
1800. St Phil PR

Ball, John Junr & Mrs. Ann Simons, 5 May 1814, at Lewis-
field, St. John. St Phil PR

Ballow, Thomas & _____ Swanston, 6 Feb 1817, by William
Capers.   Georgetown Meth Ch

Bampfield, James of Charleston, gentleman, & Harriet
Hockley Gardner, widow, 11 Dec 1816; Thomas Bampfield,
Thomas Winstanley, trustees; Peter S. Perry, John S.
Geyer, wit.   Mar Set 7: 113-115

Bampfield, James & Mrs. Harriet H. Garden, 14 Dec 1816.
St Phil PR

Bampfield, Thomas of Charleston, & Sarah Hawie, spinster,
8 April 1813; Thomas Winstanley, James Bampfield,
trustees; B. McCall, James Marsh, Peter X. Lafar, wit.
Mar Set 6: 209-212

Bampfield, Thomas & Miss Sarah Harvie, 12 April 1813, in
Charleston. St Phil PR

Bankhead, James, Colonel in U. S. Army, & Anne Pyne, daughter of John Pyne, decd., of Charleston, 23 June 1817; Honora Pyne, trustee; Mary Pyne Hutchinson, Margaret Pyne, wit.   Mar Set 7: 203-204

Banks, Thomas of Charleston, Inn-keeper, & Margery Armstrong, of Charleston, spinster, to Rev. Wm. Hollinshead, 15 March 1809.   Chaston ML

Barau, Hilaire & Marie Jeanne Heronville, 2 Nov 1816. St Mary's RC

Barbot, Antoine & Francoise Antoinette Carina Esnard, 27 March 1815.   St Mary's RC

Barfield, James & Elizabeth Davis, 18 March 1801.   Bryan Journal

Barget, John P. & Barbary Tunno, colored, 6 July 1814, in Charleston.   St Phil PR

Barksdale, George of Greenwich & Rebecca Bee Edwards of Charleston, 21 Nov 1808; James Fisher Edwards, Alexander Marion Edwards, trustees; John Gadsden, Henry M. Holmes, wit.   Mar Set 5: 440-445

Barlow, John of Newberry Dist., and wife Ann Smith, widow, 8 April 1808; William Shaw of Pendleton Dist., trustee; John Lee, John Dench, wit.   Mar Set 5: 394-396

Barnes, Jas. & Sarah Marrs, 24 Dec 1809. Bryan Journal

Barnwell, slave of D. C. Webb, Esqr., & Hager Friday, a free woman, 25 April 1816, in Cannonsborough.   St Phil PR

Barr, Daniel of Georgetown Dist., & Jannet Gregg, 10 May 1804; license directed to Rev. Duncan Brown.   Marion ML

Barr, Joseph & Eliza Houston, 1 Nov 1808. Moses Waddel

Barrentine, Wilson & Nancy McNatt, to Rev. Joshua Lewis, 5 Aug 1801.   Marlboro ML

Barrett, Judah, of Columbia, & Judith Bookter, widow of Jacob Bookter, 19 Nov 1806; Herman Kinsler, John Duke, John Campbell, wit.   Misc Rec B, pp. 446-449

Barron, Wm & Crist Colson, 23 Aug 1810. Bryan Journal

Baskin, Hugh & Sarah Brown, 27 March 1806. Moses Waddel

Baskin, John & Sarah Noble, 17 Jan 1811. Moses Waddel

Baskin, Thomas & Eliza Long, 13 March 1806. Moses Waddel

Baskins, Thomas & Mary Noble, 21 Jan 1806. Moses Waddel

Bass, Christopher & Lucy Marabel, 30 Aug 1819. Moses Waddel

Bates, James A. & Sarah Bates, 4 June 1807. Moses Waddel

Bates, Nathan & Ann Smith, 6 Jan 1814, in Charleston. St Phil PR

Batten, Richard, Newberry Dist., S. C., & Ann Cook, 1 Jan 1807. Bush R MM

Baurreus, Jean Baptiste Lur & Louisa Antoinette Pellissier, 23 March 1808. St Mary's RC

Baxter, Francis Marion & Mary Elizabeth Ervin of St. John's, Santee, 24 Nov 1809; Nathaniel Marion, trustee; Martha Warley, Jas. Shackelford, wit. Mar Set 5: 508-510

Baxter, George & Nancy Johnson, 21 Dec 1820 at Georgetown. Pr Geo Winyaw

Bay, John & Mary Wainwright, 12 Jan 1814, in Charleston. St Phil PR

Beach, Stephen and Mary Willingham(?), 12 May 1814, by A. Senter. Georgetown Meth Ch

Beall, Duke & Martha Saxon, 27 June 1811. Moses Waddel

Bearfield, James & wife Elizabeth (formerly Elizabeth Davis), 3 Sept 1803; Jesse Bearfield, trustee; Jas Wilson Jur., Richd. Singellton, wit. Mar Set 4: 359-361

Bearfield, Jesse of Colleton Dist., & Mary Hamilton of same, widow, 13 April 1803; James Bearfield, James Stevens, wit. Mar Set 5: 417-420

Bearfield, Jesse of Beaufort Dist., & Elizabeth Buchanan of same, 30 June 1813; Wm. Clark, Sarah D. Rain, wit. Mar Set 6: 255-257

Beauchamp, Elick, son of William & Elizabeth Beauchamp, Marlborough Dist., S. C., & Alice Mendenhall, daughter of Moses & Betty Mendenhall, decd., Marlborough Dist., S. C., 21 March 1811. Piney Grove MM

8

Beauchamp, William Jr., son of William & Elizabeth Beauchamp, Richmond Co., N. C., & Milley Willis, daughter
of Thomas & Lina Willis, Marlborough Co., S. C., 22
April 1802. Piney Grove MM

Bee, Barnard Elliott & Ann Wragg Fayssoux, spinster, 14
Nov 1809; James Hamilton Jr., Alfred Huger, trustees;
Joseph Winthrop, Helen Fayssoux, wit. Mar Set 5: 498-
502

Bee, Barnard-Elliott of Charleston, gentleman, & Ann-
Wragg Fayssoux, of Charleston, spinster, to Rev. James
D. Simons, 15 Nov 1809. Chaston ML

Bee, Peter Smith and wife Frances Caroline, 4 Sept 1805;
John Ward, trustee; Charles Syfan, Sappi Safan, wit.
Mar Set 5: 145-148

Beech, Ebba & Sarah Blocker, 9 Feb 1815. Bryan Journal

Beech, Thos & Nancey Costen, 25 Feb 1802. "the 25th March
next Nancey will be 12 years old". Bryan Journal

Beekman, Samuel & Susanna Bruce, of Charleston, daughter
of Thomas Smith, widow, 5 Oct 1801; Alexander Garden,
trustee; Jon Bryan, Wm. Smith Jr., wit. Mar Set 4:
98-104

Bell, Arthur & Elizabeth Foushee, 16 Oct 1816. Moses
Waddel

Bellinger, John S. of Barnwell Dist., Doctor of Physic,
& Emily Garardeau, of St. Bartholomew's Parish, widow,
8 Feb 1816; Peter Girrardeau, of St. Bartholomew's
Parish, planter, George Taylor of Coosawhatchie,
attorney at law, trustees; Sarah Baker, Peter G. Hyrne,
wit. Mar Set 7: 10-12

Belot, Jacob & Sarah Dickson, 12 May 1819. Moses Waddel

Belz, Christian-Adam of Charleston, grocer, & Barbara-
Margaret Kahnle, of Charleston, spinster, to Rev.
Faber, 1 Dec 1810. Chaston ML

Bennett, Elias Simmons & Mary W. Stiles, daughter of
Benjamin Stiles the younger, late of Stono decd., and
granddaughter of Mrs. Mary Smilie, late of Wadmalaw,
decd., 1 March 1816; Hugh Wilson, trustee; John W.
Mitchell, Joseph Burnett, wit. Mar Set 7: 35-37

Bennett, Elias Simmons of Charleston & Mary W. Stiles,
daughter of Benjamin Stiles the younger, and granddaughter of Mrs. Mary Smilie, late of Wadmalaw Island,
21 March 1816; Hugh Wilson, trustee; Anna H. Bennett,
John S. Bennett, wit. Mar Set 8: 46-50

9

Bennett, Isaac S. K. & Cath. Eliz. Faber, 21 April 1814,
in Charleston. St Phil PR

Bennett, Silas, of Anson Co., N. C., & Rebecca Easterling,
of Marlboro,   Rev. Wm. Bennett, 19 Nov 1808.   Marlboro ML

Bentham, Robert of Charleston, & Miss Frances Mayrant, 7
Dec 1819 by Rev. Parker Adams.   Holy Cross Ch

Benton, John & Eliza. Blocker, 16 July 1805.   Bryan
Journal

Benton, Mose(?) & Mary White, 20 Oct 1803.   Bryan Journal

Benton, Zac. & Eliza Barber, 15 June 1820.   Bryan Journal

Bessilleu, Mark Anthony of Charleston, mariner, & Maria
Williams, of the same place, spinster, 11 Sept 1800.
St Phil PR

Beverly, Robert, & Mary Beverly, 21 Jan 1807, to Rev. Wm.
Bennett.   Marlboro ML

Bevil, Peter & Jane Brock, 17 Dec 1818. Moses Waddel

Bibb, Benajah S. & Lucy Ann Sophia Gilmer, 19 Jan 1819.
Moses Waddel

Bibb, John D. & Mary Oliver, 6 Feb 1812. Moses Waddel

Bibb, Thomas & Pamela Thomson, __ May 1803. Moses Waddel

Bickley, John & Mary Ann Wilson, 5 June 1816. Moses
Waddel

Bickly, Waller O. Dr. & Sarah Shepherd, 10 Nov 1814.
Moses Waddel

Bigham, Samuel Maj. & Miss Mary Muldrow, license dated
13 Mar 1813; married by Daniel Smith, V. D. M., 1 Apr
1813.   Darl MB

Bird, Daniel & Sarah Oliver, 25 Dec 1806. Moses Waddel

Bishop, Jacquis, & Penelope Brockington, 29 Nov 1803;
Moses Sanders, Sec.; Jos. Woods, wit.   Darl MB

Billy, slave of Mrs. Dickson, & Emma, slave of Mrs. C.
Mitchell, 1 March 1818 in Charleston. St Phil PR

Bird, John & Elizabeth Martin, spinster, 1 Aug 1815;
Jacob Akson, trustee; Samuel Abbott, wit.   Mar Set
6: 425-426

SOUTH CAROLINA MARRIAGES 1800-1820

Bivin, John & Eleanor Mole, 28 Oct 1819. St. Mary's RC

Black, William of St. Luke's Parish, Beaufort Dist.,
planter, and wife Sarah Hanson Black, 6 April 1805;
Charles Black, trustee; Elizabeth Leacraft, John L.
Agnew, wit. Mar Set 5: 50-53

Blackman, David & Charlotte Murdy, 6 June 1811. St.
Matthews Luth Ch

Blackwell, William & Eliza Collier, 5 Dec 1816. Moses
Waddel

Blake, Daniel Esq. of Charleston, gentleman, & Anna
Louisa Middleton, of the same place, spinster, 1 Feb
1800. St. Phil PR

Blakely, Seth of Charleston & Susanna Moore of same,
widow, 24 July 1819; Thomas Ham of Village of Hamp-
stead, trustee; Christopher Twele, E. A. Lincoln, wit.
Mar Set 8: 57-58

Blamyer, William Junr. of Charleston, Factor, & Frances
Pogson, of Charleston, spinster, to Rev. James D.
Simons, 1 Nov 1809. Chaston ML

Blanding, Doctor & Miss Willet, 16 Oct 1811. Kershaw
Diary

Block, David Dr., & Mrs. _____, 26 Aug 1817 in Charleston. St. Phil PR

Blocker, _____ & Eliza. Blocker, 3 Oct 1818. Bryan
Journal

Blocker, James of Charleston & Isabella Morrison, 1 June
1812; John Blocker Jr., Abner Blocker, both of Edgefield Dist., & George Miller, trustees; Lewis A. Pit-
ray, J. C. Martindale, wit. Mar Set 6: 141-145

Blome, Cesaire & Heloise Dursse, 18 Sept 1815. St. Mary's
RC

Bob, slave of Mrs. Jas Gadsden & Rachel, slave of Mrs. B.
Allston, 12 May 1816 in St. James Goose Creek. St
Phil PR

Boddiford, Silas & Anna White, 11 Sept 1800. Bryan
Journal

Bodiford, Aaron, & Isabel McLeod, & Rev. Robert Purnell,
19 Feb 1817. Marlboro ML

11

Bold, William & Elizabeth J. Morgan, 8 Dec 1814; Margaret Munro, James Muirhead, trustees; Elizabeth G. Munro, M. King, wit.   Mar Set 6: 366-368

Boles, Isaac & Eliza Kirkwood, 14 July 1808.   Moses Waddel

Bolles, Abiel of Charleston, School-master, & Hannah Pattison, of Charleston, spinster, to Rev. Capers, 1 May 1811.   Chaston ML

Bonneau, Arnoldus of Christ Church Parish, & Martha Porcher, daughter of Peter Porcher, Esqr., decd., 20 May 1813; Joseph Palmer, Thomas Porcher, Samuel Porcher, trustees; R. McKelvey Jr., H. Ravenel Jr., wit. Mar Set 6: 222-226

Bonneau, John E. & Miss Eliza M'Credie, 8 Oct 1815 in Charleston.   St Phil PR

Bonnet, Pierre Jacques & Marianne Godesros, 21 Jan 1811. St Mary's RC

Bostick, Benjamin R. of St. Peter's Parish, Beaufort Dist., & Mary Elvira Robert, of same, granddaughter of Samuel Maner, decd., 17 June 1816; John H. Robert of same, and William H. Robert of Barnwell Dist., trustees; Elias G. Jaudon, Lucy G. Mannon, wit.   Mar Set 7: 57-59

Bouknight, Daniel & Miley Smith, 15 March 1814.   St. Michaels Luth Ch

Bouleneau, Pierre George & Marianna Poulnot, 23 Nov 1814. St. Mary's RC

Bowhay, Joseph Procter, of Charleston, butcher, & Charlotte Jarman, of the same place, spinster, 19 Jan 1802. St Phil PR

Bowles, Francis & Catharine Calhoun, 27 June 1815.   Moses Waddel

Bowman, James Junior of Beaufort, Esq., & Emily Fraser, under 21 years of age, spinster, of Walterborough; 21 Oct 1819; Alexander Fraser, M. D., & Frederick Fraser, Esq., trustees; Joseph Fraser, wit.   Mar Set 8: 75-76

Bowman, Zachariah & Nancy Goodman, _____ 1801.   Moses Waddel

Boyd, Joseph & Mary McCraven, 26 Jan 1815.   Moses Waddel

Boyd, Robert & Nancy Hutchinson, 18 Nov 1817.   Moses Waddel

Boykin, Jno. & Charlotte Mortimer, 22 April 1813.
  Kershaw Diary

Boyle, Charles of St. Paul, planter, & Mary-Ann Ryan of
  Charleston, spinster, to Rev. Thomas Mills, 19 Apr 1811.
  Chaston ML

Boylston, Henry of Charleston, M. D., and Mary E. Reid,
  5 April 1820; Robert Bentham, trustee; Thos D. Condy,
  N. H. Boylston, wit.   Mar Set 8: 110-120

Bracey, Wm. & Miss M. Rudolph, 21 Sept 1800.   Kershaw
  Diary

Bradley, Charles, of Charleston, printer, & Elizabeth
  Harvey, of the same place, spinster, 14 June 1802.
  St Phil PR

Brady, Francis of Charleston, & Martha Lafilly, widow,
  8 May 1818; Jervis Henry Stevens, Lionel H. Kennedy,
  trustee; E. Elizer, Richard W. Cogdell, wit.   Mar Set
  7: 275-277

Braid, Matthew of Charleston, carpenter, & Elizabeth
  Hudson of Charleston, spinster, 2 Feb 1815; license
  to Dr. Aaron Letan(?).   Chaston Pro J

Brailsford, Edward (Dr.) of Charleston, & Elizabeth
  Charlotte Moultrie, only daughter of William Moultrie
  Junior, late of Goose Creek decd., & Hannah Moultrie,
  widow, 25 May 1802; Gen. William Moultrie, Dr. James
  Moultrie, Solomon Legare, trustees; Sarah Elliott John-
  ston, James Hair, wit.   Mar Set 4: 153-164

Branch, _____ & Mary Marrs, 21 Sept 1813.   Bryan
  Journal

Branch, Wm. & Sarah Branes, 7 Jan 1816.   Bryan Journal

Brandeburg, Adam & Sophia Burkett, 16 Feb 1809.   St.
  Matthews Luth Ch

Brandeburg, John & Rosina Ziegler, 24 May 1810.   St.
  Matthews Luth Ch

Brandeburg, Martin & Catherine King, 5 Feb 1804.   St.
  Matthews Luth Ch

Brandt, James W. of Charleston, and wife Hannah; Sarah
  Margaret Bennett, trustee; Edward Croft, John Gist,
  John Stoney, wit.   Mar Set 4: 256-258

Brandt, Jas. W. & Miss Ann Fields of Christ Church
  Parish, 13 Dec 1815, in Charleston.   St Phil PR

Branford, Bernaby of Prince William's Parish, & Sarah
    Wilson, 14 April 1812; Richard Lubbock of St. Helena's
    Parish, trustee; Jno T. Stone, Thomas Fulton, wit.
    Mar Set 6: 252-254

Brannan, Martin & Margaret Furlong, 29 Nov 1819. St.
    Mary's RC

Brannan, Henry & Unity Loper, 10 Nov 1808.   Bryan
    Journal

Breazeal, Archibald & Dorcas Watson, 26 Oct 1809. Moses
    Waddel

Bressat, Frederic Alexandre, notary public, resident of
    Port de paix, son of Alexandre Bressat & Marie Anne
    Mohimont, native of Paris, & Marie Clair Guilmat,
    widow without children, of Pierre Posselet. proved
    23 Sept 1807. (original in French). Mar Set 5: 341-
    345

Brevoort, Henry Junr of New York City & Laura Elizabeth
    Carson, under the age of 21, daughter of Elizabeth
    Carson, 20 Sept 1817; Henry Cary, James Renwich, of
    New York, trustees; Jno J. Irvin, William Kemble, wit.
    Mar Set 7: 221-230

Brickhouse, John, & Franky Pate, to Rev. Robert Purnell,
    5 July 1818.   Marlboro ML

Bright, Basset, & Obedience Adams, to Rev. Robert Purnell,
    26 March 1818.   Marlboro ML

Bright, Purrentine, & Charlotte Easterling, to Rev.
    Robert Purnell, 1 Feb 1816.   Marlboro ML

Briton, James Henry & Caroline Delorme, 27 Dec 1820. St
    Mary's RC

Britton, Samuel of Charleston, & Elizabeth Rodgers, spin-
    ster, _____ 1813; John Baker Rodgers, trustee; Maur-
    ice Simons Jr., wit.   Mar Set 6: 283-285

Brixy, Thomas & Susan Clark, 8 Jan 1805. Moses Waddel

Broadfoot, James of Charleston, & Frances Wells, widow,
    30 Dec 1811; George McCaulay, trustee; Eliza Vincent,
    Wm. Corlett, wit.   Mar Set 6: 84-87

Brock, George & Betsy Houston, 5 Nov 1812. Moses Waddel

Brockman, Joel & Harriet Terry, 14 May 1816. Moses
    Waddel

14

Brodie, Robert of Mazyck Borough, St. Philips Parish, &
    Sarah Harriet Waring, spinster, minor daughter of Mrs.
    Harriet Waring, 7 Jan 1818; James Wilkie, John Langs-
    taff, wit. Mar Set 7: 269-271

Brooks, Benjamin of Robertville, St. Peter's Parish,
    Beaufort Dist., & Sarah Toomer, of same parish, widow
    of Thomas P. Toomer, 3 Aug 1813; Thomas Polhill Jr.,
    Elias G. Jaudon, trustees; John Robert, H. A. Boyd,
    Jas. B. Jaudon, wit. Mar Set 6: 280-283

Brooks, John F., marriner, & Jane Bishop, widow of Capt.
    Charles Bishop, marriner, 3 March 1808; John G. Thorne,
    trustee; Jane Watt, S. W. Smith, wit. Mar Set 5:
    381-385

Broome, John & Jennet Scott, widow, 2 Dec 1807; James
    McConnell, trustee; Andrew Patterson, Moses Wither-
    spoon, wit. Wmbg DB D, pp. 27-29

Brough, John & Elizabeth LeRoy, 23 Feb 1819. Moses
    Waddel

Broughton, Alexander of Charleston & Miss Caroline Bull-
    ard Harris, daughter of Dr. Tucker Harris of Charles-
    ton, 10 Dec 1810; William Clarkson, trustee; Willm A.
    Moultrie, Daniel Broughton, wit. Mar Set 6: 20-23

Broughton, Philip Porcher of St. John's Parish, Berkley,
    planter & Mary Broughton, daughter of Alexander Brough-
    ton decd., and Elizabeth Damaris Broughton, and grand-
    daughter of Elizabeth Jane Ravenel, 3 Dec 1807; Alex-
    ander Broughton, James Ravenel, trustees; Paul D.
    Mazyck, Alexr C. Mazyck, Daniel Broughton, wit. Mar
    Set 5: 354-357

Broughton, Richard L. of Parish of St. Luke & Sarah T.
    Branford, of Parish of Prince William, 31 May 1820;
    James Sharpe, Paul Ulmer, trustees; James Broughton,
    T. B. Tudor, wit. Mar Set 8: 164-166

Brown, Archibald & Miss Ann Harleston, 15 Dec 1818 in
    Mazyckborough. St Phil PR

Brown, Daniel of Barnwell Dist., minister of the gospel,
    & Harriet Porcher of same, spinster, 30 Jan 1816;
    Francis Y. Porcher, physician, of St. Peter's Parish,
    Beaufort Dist., trustee; Lau. Hext, Sarah C. Hext,
    wit. Mar Set 7: 30-32

Brown, Jeremiah & Mary Jolly, both of Pee Dee, Marion
    Dist., 26 Dec 1801; license to Revd. Mr. McCollough.
    Marion ML

Brown, Jeremiah Jr. & Ann Cusack, 7 Apr 1817. Marion ML

Brown, John of St. James Parish, carpenter, & Elizabeth Darr of Christ Church Parish, spinster, 24 March 1800; George White & Peter Darr, trustees; James Ballough, Eli Huggins, wit. Mar Set 3, pp. 443-446

Brown, Malcolm and Mary Brown (free colored persons) 7 March 1816 in Charleston. St Phil PR

Brown, Sam, & Harriet Thornton, 22 Nov 1810. Kershaw Diary

Brown, Thomas R., & Elizabeth Stroman, 4 June 1811; John Howell Junr. & Capt. Robert Hails, trustees; John A. Reese, W. R. Howell, wit. MBC Rec E, pp. 368-369

Browne, Adam J. & Miss Laura Pinckney, 19 Nov 1818 in Charleston. St Phil PR

Browne, George William, rope maker, & Mary Ann Boucheneau, spinster, 30 Jan 1802. St Phil PR

Browne, William Henri & Catherine Donovan, 6 May 1818. St Mary's RC

Bruce, Jared & Maryann Dickinson, 23 Dec 1801; Stephen Shrewsbury, trustee; Jeremiah Shrewsbury, Francis Dickinson, wit. Mar Set 4: 168-171

Brummer, Nanne & Francis Watkinson of Charleston, widow, 26 Dec 1820; John T. Vause, trustee; James G. Stoll, Philip Friedeberg, wit. Mar Set 8: 232-236

Brunson, Isham & Elizabeth McPike formerly Elizabeth Rumph, widow of Jacob Rumph, decd., 26 Aug 1819; Jonathan Brunson, trustee; Alex Fairchild, Henry Alex DeSausure, Edward Burgess, wit. Mar Set 8: 62-64

Bryan, Edward & Levicey Padget, 31 May 1808. Bryan Journal

Bryan, James & Winney Prine, 3 Nov 1811. Bryan Journal

Bryan, Jonathan of Charleston, merchant, & Sarah Latham, daughter of Daniel Latham of same, distiller, 30 April 1805; Thomas Karwon, Daniel Latham the younger, trustees; Robt Wilson, Wm. Wish, wit. Mar Set 5: 35-39

Bryan, R. J. & Ann Ulmer, 10 Feb 1814. Bryan Journal

Buchan, James & Margaret McCuloh, __ March 1820. Bryan Journal

Buchard, Henry & Magdelen Hauck, 11 May 1813. St. Matthews Luth Ch

Buchart, John & Miss Hauck, 29 May 1804. St Matthews
   Luth Ch

Buckner, Benjamin Heape & Margaret Veitch, widow of Henry
   Veitch, decd., 10 Nov 1814; Joseph Morrison, Charles
   Jones Jenkins, John Ulmer, trustees; Eleanor E. Morrison, Mary A. Morrison, John Morrison, wit. Mar Set
   6: 349-352

Budd, William of Charleston, merchant & Jane Videau
   Miller, spinster, 15 March 1817; Isaac A. Johnston,
   trustee; Robert Budd Gilchrist, R. W. Humphreys, wit.
   Mar Set 7: 143-149

Buford, William J. & Eliza M. A. Tucker, 20 Feb 1812;
   John H. Tucker, trustee; John O. Heriot, Benjn A.
   Heriot, wit. Mar Set 6: 193-196

Buford, William J. & Elizabeth Chovin, 24 March 1814;
   Hugh Fraser, trustee; Paul Michau, Alex. C. Wilks,
   wit. Mar Set 6: 320-323

Bulger, Michal & Mary McCullough, 14 Sept 1809. Bryan
   Journal

Bulit, Pierre & Marie Jeanne Dastas, 30 March 1813. St
   Mary's RC

Bulkley, Ashbel of Charleston, merchant & Ann Eliza Fanning, of Charleston, spinster, 25 May 1816. Chaston
   Pro J

Bull, Joseph & Lydia Deas (col'd persons, free) 6 April
   1815, in Charleston. St Phil PR

Bull, William Robert of Charleston, & Frances Pinckney
   Webb, 26 May 1815; Charles Webb of St. Bartholomew's
   Parish, Colleton Dist., trustee; Francis B. Fishburne,
   Peter B. Girardeau, wit. Mar Set 6: 392-405

Bull, William-Stephen, of St. Andrews, Esquire, & Rosetta
   Izard, of St. Andrews, spinster, to Rev. Thomas Mills,
   12 May 1809. Chaston ML

Burbridge, John & Elsey Brown, widow, 6 Sept 1814; Thomas
   Burbridge, trustee; Arthur Burbridge, Elisha Walling,
   Elizabeth Walling, wit. Mar Set 6: 358-360

Burden, Kinsey of Charleston, factor, & wife Mary (late
   Mary Legare), 2 Aug 1805; James Legare, Thomas Legare,
   trustees; Isaac S. Keith, Jane Keith, Thomas Burden,
   wit. Mar Set 5: 59-67

Burger, Charles & Lavinia Lesterjette, 23 Dec 1813, in
Charleston. St Phil PR

Burger, George & Miss Mary Jordan, 21 Jan 1819 in Charleston. St Phil PR

Burger, Samuel & Miss Elizabeth Gabeau, 6 Jan 1820, in
Charleston. St Phil PR

Burgoin, John & Catherine Gouth, 29 Nov 1814. St Mary's
RC

Burmeister, Jacob & Rachel Preise, 1 April 1816, in
Charleston. St Phil PR

Burn, John of Charleston, grocer, & Mary-Elizabeth Cameron, of Charleston, widow, 21 Feb 1810, to Rev. Charles
Faber. Chaston ML

Burns, Michael & Mrs. Rebecca Brown, 12 Nov 1815 in
Charleston. St Phil PR

Burrows, George William, of Charleston, mariner, & Sarah
Harvey, of the same place, widow, 24 April 1800. St
Phil PR

Butcher, Abraham, of Charleston, mariner, & Mary Gabriel,
of the same place, widow, 4 July 1801. St Phil PR

Butler, James & Miss Ann Moore Brightman, of St. James
Santee, 21 Nov 1815, in Charleston. St Phil PR

Buxbaum, John of Charleston, physician, & Eliza Ashby
Smith, spinster, 7 Dec 1820; William Greenwood the
younger of England, Robert Bentham, Martin Shobel,
trustees; Edward Frost, N. H. Boylston, wit. Mar Set
8: 201-205

Byrd, Evan of St. Bartholomew, planter, & Mary Butcher,
of Charleston, widow, to Rev. Richd. Furman, 27 Nov
1810. Chaston ML

Byrnes, Michael & Elisabeth Doyle, 1 Oct 1818. St Mary's
RC

Caldwell, Ezekiel & Sarah Shanklin, 5 Dec 1805. Moses
Waddel

Caldwell, James & Jane V. Ward, 16 Nov 1809. Moses
Waddel

Caldwell, Matthew T. & Eliza Jones, 22 Dec 1814. Moses
Waddel

Caldwell, Thomas & Mary Ward, 14 Jan 1807. Moses Waddel

Caldwell, William-Alexander of Charleston, merchant, &
Dinah Williamson, of Charleston, spinster, to Rev.
John Buchan, 11 Jan 1811. Chaston ML

Calhoun, James & Sarah C. Martin, _____ 1802. Moses
Waddel

Calhoun, John-Caldwell of Abbeville Dist., Esquire, to
Floride Colhoun, of Charleston, spinster, to Rev.
Theodore Dehon, 27 Dec 1810. Chaston ML

Calhoun, Joseph Capt. & Frances C. Darracott, 29 Jan 1819.
Moses Waddel

Calhoun, Joseph Col. & Martha Mosely, __ June 1802.
Moses Waddel

Calhoun, Patrick & Nancy De Graffenreid, 15 Dec 1803.
Moses Waddel

Calhoun, William & Catherine De Graffenreid, 30 Jan 1805.
Moses Waddel

Cambridge, James H. & wife Ann, 3 Aug 1807; Tobias Cambridge, Robert Seabrook, trustees; Thos Hewson, Thomas Richardson, wit. Mar Set 5: 357-362

Campbell, Alexander of Georgetown, & Elizabeth Hardwick
of same, widow of John Hardwick, 9 Feb 1805; Thomas
Chapman, trustee. Mar Set 4: 508-512

Campbell, Drury & Mrs. Maria An Campbell (School Mis-
tress), 7 July 1814. Kershaw Diary

Campbell, James & Martha Lee (free colored persons),
20 Nov 1814. in Charleston. St Phil PR

Campbell, Rev. John Barnwell, Beaufort, & Catharine
Amarinthea Percy, daughter of Rev. Dr. William Percy,
20 Nov 1811; James Legare, trustee; Percy Lewis, E. B.
Lining, wit. Mar Set 7: 286-290

Campbell, John-Barnwell of Beaufort Dist., Reverend, &
Catharine-Amarinetha Percy, of Charleston, spinster,
to Rev. William Percy, 20 Nov 1811. Chaston ML

Cammidge, John Dalton Junr. & Mrs. Lydia Pritchard, 28
Nov 1816 in Charleston. St Phil PR

Cannon, David & Elizabeth Clark, widow, 10 May 1804.
Bryan Journal

Cannon, Ephraim & Elenar Smith, 20 Dec 1803. Bryan
Journal

Cannon, Hugh E. & Miss Ann Muldrow, license dated 1 Oct 1809; married by James Coleman, Oct. 1809. Darl MB

Carter, Joseph & Barbara Crossby, 10 March 1809. Bryan Journal

Cannon, William Henry & Miss Sarah McTier, 12 May 1804; license directed to James Coleman. Darl MB

Cantey, Joseph Junr. of Sumter Dist., planter, & Susannah Herrington, of same, 10 May 1805; Thomas Tobias, John Herrington, trustees; James Gambrell, Moses Brogdon, Joseph Harrington, wit. Misc Rec B, pp. 368-369

Canty, John Major & Miss Emma Richardson, 7 May 1816 in Clarendon. St Phil PR

Canuet, Guillian & Susanne Giuluiany, 6 Dec 1811. St Mary's RC

Capers, Charles & Mary Capers, 12 March 1808. St Hel PR

Captain, slave of _____ & Rose, a free woman, 4 Nov 1818 in Charleston. St Phil PR

Car, Isaac of Georgetown Dist., & Sarah B. Wilson of same, 18 May 1820; William Thompson of Williamsburg District, trustee; Esther Singeltary, John P. Tamplet, wit. Mar Set 8: 134-136

Caradeus, Jean Baptiste W. Laurant & Marie Augustine Rossignole Lachicotte, 12 Nov 1811. St. Mary's RC

Carew, Edward & Esther Eve, 3 April 1811. 2d Pres Ch

Carivene, Antoine Alexis Andre & Marie Ann Luce Daudier, 28 Jan 1817. St Mary's RC

Carmichael, Daniel of Charleston, merchant, & Catharine Sarah Swift, of Charleston, widow, 11 Oct 1818; license to Revd. Dr. John Buchan. Chaston Pro J

Carmichael, Daniel, of Charleston, & wife Catherine, 26 Dec 1818; James Perry, trustee; Thomas John Gant, wit. Mar Set 8: 3-6

Carmichael, James of Charleston, & Eliza Johnston, relict of Mathew Johnston, late of Savannah, Georgia, 9 April 1805; Henry Warrell Paxton, trustee; Danl Boyter, John Ramsey, Ja. Wilson, Jno McClure Jr., wit. Mar Set 5: 16-21

Carr, Isaac & Sarah B. Wilson, 18 May 1820, at Georgetown. Pr Geo Winyaw

Carre, Pierre Andrew Parfoit & Eugenie Artus, 20 July 1815. St Mary's RC

Carrel, Joseph Jr. and Miss Martha Love, 25 March 1806, Joseph Carrel Sr., surety. York Pro 66/3118

Carrol, Delany & Judith Carr, 14 July 1810. Moses Waddel

Carrol, Ellis & Catharine Deleshaw, 24 July 1817. Moses Waddel

Carrol, Robert Ellis & Unity Harvey, 29 April 1819. Moses Waddel

Carrol, William & Rosy Grimes, 14 April 1814. Moses Waddel

Carter, Robert W. of Camden, physician & Sarah R. Dearington, a minor under 21, 24 May 1814; John Dearington, James English, trustees; John W. Whitaker, wit. Mar Set 6: 339-341

Carter, Wm. & Margaret Mills, 5 May 1803. Bryan Journal

Cary, Lemuel & Ann Hiron, widow of John Hiron decd., otherwise called Ann Delane, all of Columbia, 30 July 1807; Ainsley Hall, trustee; C. Clifton, Jane E. Perrin, wit. Misc Rec C, pp. 433-435

Casey, Thomas Dr. & Jane Noble, 21 March 1805. Moses Waddel

Casey, Thomas Dr. & Eliza Lesley, 6 Oct 1814. Moses Waddel

Cason, James & Miss Ann Louisa Cleapor, 5 Aug 1818 in Charleston. St Phil PR

Cassidy, Michael & Alley Hogan, 2 Jan 1820. St Mary's RC

Cater, Thomas M. & Sarah McPherson Postell, daughter of Mrs. Sarah Postell, 27 May 1805; James Jervey, wit. Mar Set 8: 23-27

Catterton, Mark & Anna Windon, 8 Aug 1805. Bryan Journal

Causse, Victor & Maria Susanna de Laumont, 14 Jan 1819. St Mary's RC

Chamberlain, John & Rebekah Cook, 7 April 1808. Moses Waddel

Champion, Rich'd L. & Mrs. M. E. Trent, 13 Dec 1810. Kershaw Diary

Champneys, John, of Charleston, Esqr., & Amarintha Saunders, widow of Roger Parker Saunders, 11 Dec 1800; Robert James Turnbull, attorney, & Sarah Lowndes, widow,
trustees; William Lowndes & Ebenezer Thayer, wit.
Mar Set 4: 1-9

Chancognie, Simon Jude of St. Domingo, native of Berge-
rose, dept. of Dordogne, son of Louis Charles Francois
Chancognie, and his deceased wife Montel, and Marie
Susanne Delaire, native of Rochell, dept. of Chareute,
daughter of Jacques Delaire and wife Susanne Delavergn-
ne, 20 June 1803; G. Reid, Q. U., wit. (original in
French). Mar Set 5: 199-205

Chandler, Isaac Dr., of Charleston, physician, and Catharine McCord, of the same place, widow, 20 Dec 1800.
St Phil PR

Chanler, Isaac & Catherine McCord, 15 Dec 1800; William
Clarkson & William Clarkson Jr., of Charleston, trustees; Wm. Logan Jr., wit.   Mar Set 4: 11-14

Chapeau, Jean Baptiste & Marie Pauline Leuder, 28 May
1814. St Mary's RC

Charbonnier, Joseph Claude & Therese Margaret Touris,
24 Aug 1811. St Mary's RC

Charles, slave of Mrs. James Hamilton, & Mary, slave of
Mrs. Moodey, 28 April 1814, in Charleston. St Phil PR

Charles, slave of Mr. William Trescott & Isabella, slave
of Mr. T. W. Bacot, 15 May 1817 in Charleston. St
Phil PR

Charles, Henry & Mrs. Ann Bow, 30 Oct 1814, in Charleston. St Phil PR

Chartrand, John of Mantanzas, Cuba, residing in Charles-
ton, & Louisa Dubois, daughter of Louis Dubois, 28
April 1820; Francis Laborde, Louis Dubois, trustees;
Henry Grimke, M. King, wit.   Mar Set 8: 122-125

Chasal, Jean Pierre & Elisabeth Caroline Anne Delalande,
8 Feb 1814. St Mary's RC

Cheesborough, John W. & Eliza Stone, 5 Dec 1816, at
Georgetown.   Pr Geo Winyaw

Cheesborough, William C. & Elizabeth Smith of Georgetown,
___ May 1806; Robert Smith of Charleston District,
Robert F. Withers, trustees; Elizabeth F. Blyth, wit.
Mar Set 5: 284-286

Cheesebrough, John W. of Georgetown Dist., & Eliza Stone, of Philadelphia, 13 Nov 1816; Richard Shackelford, Thomas Carr, of Georgetown Dist., trustees; M. L. Shackelford, M. P. Allston, wit. Mar Set 7: 170-175

Chertraud, John & Louisa Dubois, 29 April 1820. St. Mary's RC

Chevard, Pierre Desire, French citizen, native of Chartres, Dept. d"eure et Loire, son of Vincent Chevard, notary public in Chartres, & Dme Marie Madelaine Saintsot, and Marie Rose Antoinette Michel, daughter of Dam Marie Margueritte Baussaure, widow of Jean Bastiste Ignace Michel, of St. Domingo, 5 June 1801. (original in French, translated BHH). Mar Set 4: 66-69

Chinners, George Washington of Charleston, Esqr., and wife Sarah Ann Elizabeth; Archibald McDowell of Charleston, trustee; John Readhimer, Saml Huff, wit. Mar Set 5: 159-162

Chinners, Hardy H. of Charleston Dist., & Sarah Ann Elizabeth Chinners, 12 Nov 1818; William Ehney, trustee; William Hamlin, Mary Ehney, wit. Mar Set 7: 298-301

Chisolm, Robert & Mrs. Mary Evans, widow of William Evans decd. of Edisto Island, 25 May 1803; William Edings, trustee; Andrew Kerr, Margt Kerr, wit. Mar Set 4: 312-319

Choignard, Charles & Catherine Elmore, 22 Sept 1803; John Oeland, trustee; Lewis Monna, wit. Mar Set 4: 319-323

Chouler, Joseph & Mary Brune, of Charleston, widow of Derdrick Julius Brune, late of New York, 16 June 1803; George Peters of Charleston, trustee; Thos Mills, Walter Shaw, wit. Mar Set 4: 346-357

Church, Slocum, of Charleston, carpenter, & Mary McDonald of the same place, spinster, 28 June 1801. St Phil PR

Ciples, Lewis & Sarah Adamson, 13 June 1811. Kershaw Diary

Clanet, Peter of Charleston, Saddler, & Mary Dowen, of Charleston, spinster, to Rev. Richd. Furman, 1 Jan 1810. Chaston ML

Clark, James of Charleston, mariner, & Mary Simonson, of the same place, widow, 27 Nov 1800. St Phil PR

Clark, Jonathan, son of John & Margaret Clark, decd., Guilford Co., N. C. & Ruth Moorman, daughter of Zachariah & Mary Moorman, Marlborough Co., S. C., 25 March 1802. Piney Grove MM

Clark, Mark D. & Nancy Norman, 2 July 1818. Moses Waddel

Clark, Mathew, of St. Paul's Parish, planter, & Mary _____, of the same place, spinster, 18 Dec 1800. St Phil PR

Clay, John & Elizabeth Covin, 15 April 1812. Moses Waddel

Clement, William, of Charleston, attorney, & Sarah, youngest daughter of Morten Wilkinson, late of St. Paul's Parish, planter (already married), 2 March 1801; Charles Derndas Deas, merchant, trustee; Wm. Yeadon, John B. Campbell, wit. Mar Set 4: 33-36

Coat, Samuel, son of Marmaduke Coat, & Margaret Coppock, 8 May 1800. Bush R MM

Coate, Henry Capt. Esqr., & Betsy Long, daughter of Capt. Benjamin Long, Esqr., all of Newberry District, bond dated 27 Jan 1803. Minister's return by Rev. John Boulger, 30 Jan 1803. Newberry Will Book C, pp. 460-462

Coate, James, son of Marmaduke Coate, Newberry Dist., S. C., & Mary Miles, 29 Oct 1800. Bush R MM

Coate, William, son of Marmaduke Coate, Newberry Dist., S. C., & Elizabeth Miles, 29 June 1800. Bush R MM

Coates, Joseph S. & Eliza Scott, 2 Nov 1819; James Haig, John M. Righton, trustees; Samuel Yates, J. E. Yates, trustees. Mar Set 8: 84-88

Cobb, Thomas W. & Polly W. Moore, 14 May 1807. Moses Waddel

Cobia, Francis-Joseph of Charleston, butcher, & Ann Fletter, of Charleston, spinster, to Rev. Charles Faber, 28 Feb 1811. Chaston ML

Cochran, David & Miss Lotitia Cochran, 17 Nov 1816 in Charleston.

Coe, William H. & Mary Adeline Coachman, 9 Nov 1820; Henry McNish, trustee; William W. Morgan, Joseph B. Armstrong, wit. Mar Set 8: 178-180

Cofer, Thomas L. & Eliza Clark, 25 Jan 1810. Moses Waddel

Coggeshell, James C. & Margaret Priot, 28 Jan 1819 at
  Georgetown. Pr Geo Winyaw

Cohen, Barnett of Barnwell Dist., & wife Bella, 19 Oct
  1814; Timothy Street, John C. Allen, trustees; Elias
  Abrahams, Michael Simpson, wit. Mar Set 6: 345-349

Cohen, Nathan of Charleston & Christiana Brower, widow,
  9 Jan 1806; Jervis Henry Stevens, trustee; Jas. G.
  Singletary, Hannah Cohen, Celia Cohen, wit. Mar Set
  5: 155-159

Cole, John of Charleston, mariner, & Eliza-Luther Bennett
  of Charleston, spinster, to Rev. Richd. Furman, 2
  March 1809. Chaston ML

Cole, Mason G. & Harriet Duke, 6 Oct 1816, Richland Dist.;
  Daniel Perry, Eliza Donnavan, wit. Misc Rec C, pp.
  442-445

Coles, Isaac & Sally Walls, 22 Nov 1810. Moses Waddel

Collins, Alexander of Georgetown, & Elizabeth Skinner,
  widow, of Georgetown Dist., 17 Dec 1807; George
  Skinner, trustee; Francis M. Baxter, wit. Mar Set
  7: 101-103

Collins, Charles Henri of Beaufort Dist., & Ann Mary
  Robarts, 17 Jan 1816; Abraham Isaac Robarts, Esq.,
  father of Ann Mary, trustee; Edmd Martin, wit. Mar
  Set 7: 75-77

Colman, Benjamin & Ollivette Cotal, 4 Oct 1813. St
  Mary's RC

Colman, William, now residing in the town of Beaufort &
  Elizabeth C. Lawrence, widow, 29 June 1815; William
  Joyner, Stephen Lawrence, Samuel Lawrence, trustees;
  James Ellis, Edward J. Grayson, wit. Mar Set 6:
  387-389

Colson, George & Elizer Ann Parker, 1 Dec 1814. Bryan
  Journal

Comalander, John & Margaret Nichols, 22 June 1820. Drehr
  Journal

Commander, Samuel of Georgetown Dist., & Elizabeth Vereen,
  widow of same, 7 May 1812; Nathan Huggins, Robert
  Huggins, trustees; J. M. Atkinson, wit. Mar Set 6:
  121-123

Connolly, Jeremiah of Charleston, mariner, & Mary-Haly
  Connolly, of Charleston, widow, to Rev. James D. Simons,
  2 May 1810. Chaston ML

Connor, Frederic & Sarah Bradford, 28 Sept 1815. Moses
    Waddel

Contador, Dn. Gonzalo Zamorano, & Da. Ana Dupont, of
    Charleston, 6 Oct 1800. (original in Spanish). Mar
    Set 4: 240-241

Conyers, James of Sumter Dist., & Martha Montgomery,
    widow of William Montgomery, of same, 24 Aug 1804;
    Charles F. Lesesne, H. Bennett, trustees; Daniel
    McDonald, Rachel McDonald, William Hilton, wit.
    Misc Rec B, pp. 341-342

Coogler, Mathias & Elizabeth Weed, 20 Feb 1820. Drehr
    Journal

Cook, Joseph B. Rev. & Eleanor Walker, 6 June 1801; Cor-
    nelius DuPre & William Walker, of Georgetown, trustees;
    Sarah D. Laborn, Mary E. DuPre, William Grant, wit.
    Mar Set 4: 87-91

Cook, William, son of Isaac & Sarah Cook, Union Dist.,
    & Sarah Hawkins, daughter of John & Mary Hawkins, 10
    Oct 1805. Cane Cr MM

Coppley, Elias of St. Mark, planter, to Dianah Young
    Brimner, of Charleston, spinster, to Rev. William
    Percy, 27 Feb 1809. Chaston ML

Corasey, Michael & Catherine Powers, 24 Jan 1806; John
    McCarthy, trustee; Jno St. Clair, wit. Mar Set 5:
    140-141

Corderay, Thomas of Charleston, grocer, & Mrs. Ann Booner,
    20 Jan 1816; James Harper, trustee; Benj. R. Porter,
    Robt Brodie Jr., wit. Mar Set 6: 426-431

Couturier, Elias & Miss Susan A. Gilliland, 4 Feb 1819 in
    Charleston. St Phil PR

Couturier, Isaac, the younger of Parish of St. John Berk-
    ley, planter, & Eliza Maria Laurence, widow, 18 March
    1813; Thomas Mathews, John Fraser, trustees; John W.
    Mathews, Anna R. Couturier, wit. Mar Set 6: 248-251

Covin, Peter & Delilah Bryan, 16 Feb 1809. Moses Waddel

Covington, John W. & Elizabeth Strother, to Rev. Joshua
    Lewis, 2 Apr 1807. Marlboro ML

Covington, Richard & Caroline Bickly, 5 May 1814. Moses
    Waddel

Cowan, John, of Charleston, rigger, and Maria Basilleau,
    of the same place, widow, 25 May 1802. St Phil PR

Cowen (Corven?), Lieut. Wm. & Mrs. Charlotte Lesesne, by Jos. Travis, 24 Nov 1813. Georgetown Meth Ch

Cowing, Henry, of Charleston, merchant, & Ann Wagner, of Charleston, spinster, 3 March 1813; license to Right Reverend Dr. Theodore Dehon. Chaston Pro J

Cox, James, of Charleston, merchant, & Elizabeth Bonneau of same, spinster, daughter of Francis Bonneau, decd., 4 Oct 1802; Sarah Eleanor Bonneau, Joseph Johnson, trustees; Henry Bailey, Geo Robt Logan, wit. Mar Set 4: 219-229

Coxson, Thomas D. & Sarah Bond, persons of color, 1 Feb 1819 in Charleston. St Phil PR

Crafts, William, the elder of Charleston, & Harriet Beresford Poaug of Charleston, widow, 17 Sept 1810; Alexander Inglis, George Clitherall of N. C., W. Crafts Jr., trustees; Mary Inglis, Geo. Hy. Inglis, wit. Mar Set 6: 107-110

Crafts, William Senr. of Charleston, Esquire, & Harriet-Beresford Poaug, of Charleston, widow, 18 Sept 1810. Chaston ML

Craig, James & Rosannah Gray, 18 April 1805. Moses Waddel

Cranmer, James & Mary McFarland, 12 Dec 1805. Moses Waddel

Craven, James & Ann Loper, 25 Oct 1810. Bryan Journal

Crawford, William & Charlotte Allen, 15 Nov 1810. Moses Waddel

Crean, John & Adelaide Rene, 12 Nov 1812. St Mary's RC

Crews, Roger & Eliza. Mitchell, 27 Sept 1808. Bryan Journal

Crews, Samuel & Susanna Johnson, 26 Jan 1804. Bryan Journal

Crews, Stephen & Nancy Bradley, 30 Nov 1815. Bryan Journal

Cripp, Octavius of Charleston & Esther Deliesseline, spinster, daughter of Francis G. Deliesseline and wife Ann, 11 April 1816; Francis A. Deliesseline of Camden, trustee; J. B. White, Hugh P. Dawes, wit. Mar Set 7: 43-47

Cripps, Octavius & Esther Allston Deliesseline, 11 April 1816, at Charleston. Pr Geo Winyaw

Crocker, Elhanon & Elizabeth Young, Laurens Dist., 11 Nov
1815; Josiah Fowler, trustee; Richard Fowler, James
Medley, wit.   Misc Rec C, pp. 229-230

Croft, Edward Esqr., of Charleston, barrister at law, &
Florida Lydia Gaillard, 11 Nov 1802; John Gaillard,
Theodore Gaillard, Francis G. Deliesseline, Esqrs.,
trustees; Peyre Gaillard, Elizabeth Randol, wit.   Mar
Set 4: 231-232

Crofts, Peter & Marry Allen, both of Georgetown Dist.,
6 Feb 1817, by Sam. Hodges. Georgetown Meth Ch

Cross, George Warren of Charleston, & Mary Man Pawley,
spinster, daughter of Mrs. Sarah Mackie, widow, 28
Nov 1807; John Julius Pringle, John Dawson Jr., trustees.   Mar Set 5: 362-368

Cross, Henry & Miss Mary Ann Williams, 4 Nov 1819 in
Charleston. St Phil PR

Crossby, Aaron & Elizabeth Steedler, 31 Dec 1807. Bryan
Journal

Crossby, Daniel & Edey Thomas, 16 Dec 1811. Bryan Journal

Crossby, Henry & Mary Carter, 21 June 1808. Bryan Journal

Crossby, Jacob & Peggy Smith, 1 Sept 1808. Bryan Journal

Crossby, Wm & Rachel Herndon, 26 Oct 1808. Bryan Journal

Crouch, Abraham & Jane S. Withers (already married), 15
July 1806; Mary Ancrum Walker, mother of Jane S. With-
ers, trustee; S. Quince, J. Edwards, John Holland, wit.
Mar Set 5: 225-228

Crouch, Richd. F. & Eliza D. Simons, 9 Jan 1820. Bryan
Journal

Crow, Edward & Miss Eliza Hislop, 8 Feb 1817 in Charleston. St Phil PR

Crow, John of Charleston & Margaret Shaw, of same, 9 Dec
1803; David McKelvey, wit.   Mar Set 4: 357-359

Crowell, Jeremiah & Sarah Dewees, 29 Jan 1806; Samuel
Rodgers, trustee; John DeBow, Phins. Parker, wit.
Mar Set 5: 163-165

Crumton, (Henry T.?) & Matilda S. Bryan, 23 Dec 1819.
Bryan Journal

Crumton, John & Mary A. Ulmer, 4 Dec 1817. Bryan
Journal

Cuffee, slave of Mrs. Eliza Billing & Nelly, slave of Mrs.
Aiken, 12 Nov 1814, in Charleston. St Phil PR

Cuffy, slave of James Cook & Lucy, slave of Miss Susan
Fraser, 31 Aug 1813, in Charleston. St Phil PR

Cummins, ____ & Isabel Lowry, 30 Sept 1806. Moses
Waddel

Cunningham, Thos & Polly Hamilton, 8 March 1810. Moses
Waddel

Cuthbert, John Alexander & Mary Williamson, 15 Dec 1811.
St Hel PR

Dabbs, Jesse & Eliza Rogers, _____ 1801. Moses Waddel

Daise, Jas. & Miss Marg. Chesnut, 9 Nov 1808. Kershaw
Diary

Dangerris, Luois & Marguerite Daste, 29 Nov 1814. St
Mary's RC

Darracott, Herbert & Floride Turnbull, 20 March 1817.
Moses Waddel

Darrell, John Smith & Miss Elizabeth Browne Lequeux,
Christ Church Parish, 16 Nov 1809; Jos. Dubose, Saml
Dubose, wit. Mar Set 5: 522-523

Darrell, Nicholas Capt. & Mrs. Mary McDougal, both of
Charleston, 9 Aug 1800. St Phil PR

David, slave of Mr. Robertson & Sarah, slave of Miss
Bowman, 30 Dec 1815, in Charleston. St Phil PR

Davis, Garah & Peggy Ellis, 13 Nov 1801. Moses Waddel

Davis, James & Sarah Dickinson (free persons of color)
14 June 1815, in Charleston. St Phil PR

Davis, John of Charleston, merchant, & Martha Moubray, of
Charleston, spinster, to Rev. James D. Simons, 2 Jan
1809. Chaston ML

Davis, John W. of Georgetown, and Ann Eliza McIver, of
Darlington Dist., daughter of John McIver decd, 20
July 1806; David R. Williams, of Darlington District,
trustee. Mar Set 5: 252-257

Davis, Moses & Hannah Deleiben, widow, 23 March 1813;
Jacob Lazarus, Bella Hart, widow, trustees; N. Emanuel,
Levy Moses, Jane Hart, wit. Mar Set 6: 191-193

SOUTH CAROLINA MARRIAGES 1800-1820

Davis, Robert & Jane Gray, 23 March 1809. Moses Waddel

Davis, Thomas & Ann Oats, 12 July 1812.   2d Pres Ch

Dawson, Lawrence Monk of Charleston, & Miss Jane Vander-
    horst, daughter of Gen. Arnoldus Vanderhorst, 31 March
    1812; Elias Horry, John Stanyarne Vanderhorst, & Elias
    Vanderhorst, trustees; Danl Jas Ravenel, Saml Burger,
    wit. Mar Set 6: 126-127

Dawson, William, M. D., and Miss Caroline Prioleau, 29
    Dec 1802. St Phil PR

Deas, Jas. & Miss Mary Chesnut, 9 Nov 1808. Kershaw
    Diary

Deas, William & Ann Timothy (free people of color), 7
    Oct 1812, in Charleston. St Phil PR

Deas, William Allen & wife Ann, 19 April 1803; Henry
    Izard, David Deas, trustees; Chs. D. Deas, Seaman
    Deas, wit. Mar Set 4: 301-303

DeCottes, Alphonse Louis & Anne Constance Laffiteau, 15
    Jan 1814. St Mary's RC

DeCottes, Louis Jean Baptiste & Rose Adelaide Talvande,
    3 Oct 1815. St Mary's RC

Dehon, Right Revd. Theodore, D. D., & Sarah Russell, 26
    Oct 1813, in St. Philip's Church. St Phil PR

Deickert, J. G. and wife Rebecca, daughter of William
    Corrill, decd., late of Christ Church Parish, 3 Feb
    1806; John Russell, Henry Bartless, wit. Mar Set 5:
    197-199

Delane, Freeman of Richland Dist., physician, & Ann
    Hirons of same, 22 March 1803; Isaac Tucker of same,
    Esqr., trustee; J. M. Howell, James Adams, wit.
    Misc Rec B, pp. 214-217

Delaney, William & Martha Grimes, 16 Feb 1815. Moses
    Waddel

Delettre, William Albert & Marie Marlous Rasegnol, 1 May
    1813. St Mary's RC

Della Torre, Antonio & Margaret Ann Ryan, 8 June 1816.
    St Mary's RC

Demry, John & Mary Hardwick, 12 June 1809. Marion ML

Denison, Dr. Henry & Hannah C. Waldo, 14 May 1817 at
    Georgetown. Pr Geo Winyaw

30

Denny, Thomas of Charleston, physician, & Mary Deborah
    Lee Gowdey, spinster, 14 Nov 1803; David Johnston,
    Samuel Prioleau Junr., trustees; Thomas G. Prioleau,
    wit.   Mar Set 4: 445-455

Dent, James and Miss Catharine Cooper, 27 Feb 1817 in St.
    Philip's. St Phil PR

Depass, Joseph, & Hannah Hart, aged 18 years, 15 Jan 1813;
    Simon Moses Hart, guardian; Nathaniel G. Cleary, trust-
    ee; Es. Levy, Charles Fraser, wit.   Mar Set 6: 169-
    174

Derby, Robert of Charleston, taylor, & Rebecca Sinclair,
    of the same place, 23 Oct 1800. St Phil PR

Dervmas, Francois & Maria Eugenie Lalaiie, 27 Dec 1819.
    St Mary's RC

DeSaussure, Henry Alexander & Susan Boone, spinster,
    both of Charleston, 18 Dec 1810; Thomas Boone, Honble
    Henry Wm. DeSaussure, trustees; Maria Fraser, George
    Fraser, wit.   Mar Set 6: 11-16

Despugot, Louis Passailaigue & Marie Eulalie Caije, 30
    Aug 1814. St Mary's RC

Deveaux, Thomas & Jane Porteous, 6 June 1805; John
    Porteous, trustee; Benjn Fuller, Edward Barnwell Jr.,
    Joshua Fewox, wit.   Mar Set 5: 25-27

Dewees, John of Charleston, & Hannah Hamlin of Christ
    Church Parish, 28 Oct 1818; John White, William De-
    wees Jr., trustees; John Hamlin, Jos. Dewees, wit.
    Mar Set 7: 302-304

Dewitt, Charles & Phebee Crossby, 8 Aug 1808.   Bryan
    Journal

Dewitt, Charles & Mary Blocker, 11 April 1816.   Bryan
    Journal

Deye, Benjamin & Susan O'Donall, 6 July 1820.   St Mary's
    RC

Diaz, Antonio & Maria Tordes, 21 Aug 1816.   St Mary's RC

Dick, slave of Mrs. Logan & Sarah Vardell, free woman of
    color, 11 Aug 1820 in Charleston. St Phil PR

Dickerson, Henry H. & Miss Martha Brevard, 1 Dec 1808.
    Kershaw Diary

Dickey, John & Agnes Baird, 21 Nov 1816.   Moses Waddel

Dickson, Sterling & Mary A. Noble, __ 1801. Moses Waddel

Diggs, Little Berry, son of William & Fanny Diggs, Anson
Co., N. C., & Lydia Way, daughter of William & Abigail
Way, Marlborough Dist., S. C., 21 March 1811. Piney
Grove MM

Dilgar, Jacob R. of St. Bartholomew's Parish, & Susannah
L. Hughes, widow, _____ 1812; Bartley Ferguson of
Prince Williams Parish, & Arthur Hughes of St. Bartholomew's Parish, trustees; Ann Ferguson, Ann Carlton,
wit. Mar Set 6: 369-371

Dilgar, Jacob R. of St. Bartholomew's Parish and Francis
McCants, 2 Dec 1819; William Osward, trustee; Alfred
Walton, James S. Miles, Richard Singleton, wit. Mar
Set 8: 93-94

Dimmery, John & Mary Hardeek, 12 June 1809; John Smith
of Marion Court House, sec. Marion ML

Discombe, James-Haydon, of Charleston, Taylor, & Eliza
Ann Cleary, of Charleston, spinster, 11 Aug 1808, to
Rev. Richd. Furman. Chaston ML

Dobson, Oliver L. of Savannah, Ga., & Harriet Mathews of
Charleston, spinster, _____ 1818; John K. Mathews,
trustee; Maria Brisbane, Wm. Mathews, wit. Mar Set
7: 296-298

Domingete, Francois Denis & Catherine Marchand, 16 April
1816. St Mary's RC

Doudge, Smith, & Elizabeth Bright, Rev. Robert Purnell,
20 Nov 1820. Marlboro ML

Doughty, Dr. James & Sarah B. Pawley, 17 Dec 1818, at
Georgetown. Pr Geo Winyaw

Dove, William P. & Sarah Flint, 15 Sept 1812, in Charleston. St Phil PR

Dowdney, Thomas of Georgetown, & Rebecca Villepontoux,
of same, 31 Dec 1807; William Grant, trustee; Paul
Michau Jr., wit. Mar Set 7: 109-112

D'Oyley, Charles W. of Charleston, & Sarah Eliza Baker,
of St. Bartholomew's Parish, spinster, 14 April 1817;
George Taylor, of Coosawhatchie, attorney, trustee;
John S. Bellinger, Susan P. Webb, wit. Mar Set 7:
158-160

Doyley, C. M. and Miss Baker, 15 April 1817 in St. Bartholomew's. St Phil PR

Drayton, Dr. Charles & Miss Mary Shoolbred, daughter of
James Shoolbred of Charleston, 11 May 1813; Wilmot S.
Gibbes, John Middleton, trustees; Robert A. Gibbes,
Henry Alexr. DeSaussure, wit.   Mar Set 6: 240-247

Drayton, John & Hester Rose, daughter of Philip Tidyman,
20 May 1802; Philip Tidyman, Susan Tidyman, wit.   Mar
Set 4: 171-177

Drege, Pierre & Margueritte Colzy, 3 Feb 1816.   St Mary's
RC

Drehr, David & Rebekah Shular, 21 Oct 1819.   Drehr Journal

Drehr, Godfrey, son of John and Ann Drehr, & Catharine
Miller, daughter of Revd R. J. Miller, 13 Dec 1810.
St. Michaels Luth Ch

Drew, George Capt. & Miss Maria E. Cleapor, 15 Feb 1818,
in Charleston.   St Phil PR

Drewes, Henry of Charleston, & Magdalena Wilson, widow,
23 July 1812; John Schwartz, John Strohecker, trustees;
Lionel H. Kennedy, John S. Cogdell, wit.   Mar Set 6:
153-155

Dubart, Philip & Polly Bernart (Bernhart), 10 Feb 1820.
Drehr Journal

Dubose, Henry of Sumter Dist., & Elizabeth McKewn, spinster, of St. George's Parish, Colleton Dist., 31 Dec
1818; Archibald McKewn, trustee; Mary Lowrey, Charles
Lowrey, wit.   Mar Set 7: 316-318

Dubose, Samuel & Miss Jane Dick, 19 July 1809.   Darl MB

Dubose, Samuel Junr. of St. Stephen, planter, & Eliza
Marion, of St. Stephen, spinster, 1 June 1808.
Chaston ML

Dufort, John & Marie Gertrude Pellissier, 20 May 1809.
St Mary's RC

Duhadway, Caleb-Brown, of Charleston, Sadler, & Catharine
Hoban, of Charleston, spinster, 4 Nov 1808, to Rev.
Wm. Hollinshead.   Chaston ML

Duignan, Michael & Bridget McDonald, 5 Jan 1820.   St
Mary's RC

Dunnum, Thomas of Georgetown Dist., & Mary Anderson,
widow of Alexander Anderson, 17 Jan 1804; Alexander
Collins, Thomas Ballow, trustees; Sarah Handlin, Thos
J. Jas. Dupree, wit.   Mar Set 4: 395-398

DuPont, John & Mary Colley Stent, widow, of Charleston, 10 Nov 1802; Abraham Seaver, trustee; John C. Huaff, Saml O. Parker, wit. Mar Set 4: 325-334

DuPuy, Louis Thomas & Marie Ponse, 18 Nov 1809. St Mary's RC

Duquererois, Francois M. & Rene Antoinette Planquet, 11 June 1815. St Mary's RC

Durban, Ambroise & Agatha Fengeurs, 10 Dec 1811. St Mary's RC

Duval, Joseph, aged 27, native of La Croix des Bouquets, port au Prince, Island of St. Domingo, & Miss Elizabeth Ballon, aged 15 years, daughter of Andrew Ballon, of Charleston, 2 Jan 1812; Charles Tew, John Fredk. Kern, J. C. Custor, Frans. Cheramy, wit. Mar Set 6: 88-89

Duval, Joseph & Elizabeth Ballon, 9 Jan 1812. St Mary's RC

Dwyer, Samuel & Elizabeth Dubose, both of Sumter Dist., 3 June 1820; Caleb Rembert, trustee; Blake Robinson, E. G. Brown, wit. Misc Rec D, pp. 198-201

Early, Andrew & Barbara Staggers, both residing in Williamsburg County, 6 May 1800; Samuel Malcomson, & James Burgess, trustees; John Carrth, Wm. Gamble, wit. Mar Set 3: 448-450

Easterling, James & Sarah Manship, to Rev. Wm. Bennett, 23 Dec 1813. Marlboro ML

Easterling, Joel & Obedience Adams, to Rev. Daniel McKay, 21 March 1817. Marlboro ML

Earles, Oswald & Nancey Green, 24 Dec 1801. Bryan Journal

Eccles, Rev. Samuel & Ann Pettigrew of Darlington Dist., widow of Alexander Pettigrew, 21 Apr 1808; Timothy Dargan & Col. William Zimmerman, trustees; Jno. D. Orr, Jos. Woods, Wm Connell, wit. Misc Rec. B, pp. 498-505

Eckhard, Jacob, the younger of Charleston, gentleman, & Elizabeth Strobel, of same, spinster, daughter of Daniel Strobel, decd., 9 Nov 1814; Abraham Markley, trustee. Mar Set 6: 343-345

Eckoff, George W. of Charleston, & Catharine Kennitzs, of same, widow, 20 May 1818; James Maine, trustee; Wm. Kunhardt, John Doughty, wit. Mar Set 7: 295-296

Eden, Jonah of Christ Church Parish, & Ann Miles Joy of
    St. James Parish, 14 May 1804; Childermas Crofts,
    trustee; James Joy, Benjn Smith, wit.   Mar Set 4: 405-
    407

Edward, James & Sarah Tittle, 24 Dec 1811.   Moses Waddel

Edwards, Edward A. & Miss Mary C. Elliott, 31 Jan 1815,
    in Charleston.   St Phil PR

Edwards, Edward H. & Miss Frances Elliott, 25 Feb 1818 in
    Charleston.   St Phil PR

Edwards, George of Beaufort Dist., planter, & Elizabeth
    Barksdale, daughter of Thomas Barksdale, Esqr., late
    of Christ Church Parish, decd., 1 June 1801; Thomas
    Harrison McCalla, physician, trustee; Henry Bond,
    Eliza Edwards, wit.   Mar Set 4: 45-52

Edwards, James Fisher & Miss Mary Edwards Gadsden, 30
    May 1816 in Mazyckborough.   St Phil PR

Ehney, Peter M. of Charleston, & Sarah Roper Rose, dau-
    ghter of Jeremiah Rose, of same, 15 Dec 1804; William
    Ehney, trustee; Anna Rose, Alexr Thompson, wit.   Mar
    Set 4: 481-485

Eiglebarger, John & Elizabeth Roof, 7 Oct 1819.   Drehr
    Journal

Elders, William & Mary Boucher, Richland Dist., 13 Jan
    1816; John Elders, Thomas Wescoat, wit.   Misc Rec C,
    pp. 222-223

Elfe, William, factor & commission merchant, of Charles-
    ton & Sarah Ann Legare, 21 Dec 1818; Robert Primrose,
    Maurice Simons, trustees; Thomas H. Edwards, Isaac
    Elfe, wit.   Mar Set 8: 31-34

Elfe, William & Miss Sarah Legare, 29 Dec 1818 in St.
    Philip's church.   St Phil PR

Eli, slave of Mrs. Jas. Ladson, & Diana, slave of Mrs.
    Marchant, 19 March 1818 in Charleston.   St Phil PR

Ellerbe, William F. & Elizabeth Robertson, to Rev. Joshua
    Lewis, 28 Dec 1807.   Marlboro ML

Elliott, Barnard of Charleston, and wife Juliet Georgiana,
    7 April 1800; Robert Gibbes, Lewis Gibbes, trustees;
    Daniel E. Huger, William Lowndes, wit.   Mar Set 5:
    431-437

Elliott, Benjamin of Charleston, Esquire, & Catharine-
Osborn Savage, of Charleston, spinster, to Rev. Theodore Dehon, 7 May 1810. Chaston ML

Ellis, Elisha & Phebe Gale, _____ 1800. Moses Waddel

Ellis, Richard of St. Helena Parish, & Sarah Witter, of
same, daughter of Jonathan Witter, 4 Oct 1814; David
Turner, Robert De Treville, trustees; Paul A. Cartwright, Edmund Ellis, James Hogg, wit. Mar Set 6:
341-343

Ellis, Samuel, planter & Mary Jeannerett, of St. James
Santee, 16 Aug 1800; Abraham Michau, planter, trus-
tee; Isaac Michau, Catharine Jeannerett, wit. Mar
Set 3: 492-494

Ellis, Thomas of Charleston, bricklayer, & Mary Green, of
Charleston, spinster, 9 Oct 1811. Chaston ML

Ellison, William, attorney at law, of Edgefield Dist.,
& Ann Catharine Thomson of Charleston, spinster, 8 May
1813; George Warren Cross, James Jervey, John F. Trezevant, trustees; Charlotte Cross, Harriet Halsey, wit.
Mar Set 6: 213-218

Ellison, William & Miss Ann Thompson, of St. Michael's
Congregation, 10 May 1813, in Charleston. St Phil PR

Elstob, Simon, painter of Charleston, & Elizabeth, his
wife, 1 Jan 1800; Archibald Brebner, trustee; Edward
Croft, Henry Lenud, wit. Mar Set 3, pp. 427-429

English, John & Eliz. Tucker, 12 June 1800. Kershaw
Diary

Ervin, James, Esquire, attorney at law, & Eliza M. Witherspoon; license directed to Revd. Duncan Brown, 31
May 1805. Marion ML

Erwin, James Daniel & Sarah Frunier Sabb, 4 Feb 1811.
St Matthews Luth Ch

Evans, Daniel, & Alsey Edwards, of Marlboro, to Rev.
Robert Purnell, 8 Oct 1817. Marlboro ML

Evans, George, of St. Paul, physician, & Sarah-Bolton
Villepontoux, of Charleston, spinster, to Rev. William Percy, 30 Oct 1810. Chaston ML

Evans, Henry M. of St. Pauls Parish, and Martha Rivers of
James Island, 18 Sept 1805; Francis Rivers the elder
and Francis Rivers the younger of James Island, trustees; Wm Grant, wit. Mar Set 5: 84-90

Evans, Robert, son of Robert Evans, Newberry Dist., &
Kerenhappock Gaunt, 28 Feb 1805. Bush R. MM

Evans, Thomas Col. of Marlboro, & Wilhelmina Amelia
Charlotte Stewart, of Darlington, to Rev. Joshua Lewis,
2 March 1800. Marlboro ML

Evans, Thomas, Esq., & Rebecca Dewitt of Marlboro Co.,
to Rev. Joshua Lewis, 1 Dec 1803. Marlboro ML

Evans, William & Susan Gabeau, 2 July 1814, in Charleston.
St Phil PR

Eveleigh, George of the Dist. of Sumter, & Ann Walker of
St. John's Parish, Charleston Dist., 15 Dec 1808;
Charles Sinkler, Charles Richardson, trustees; William Sinkler, Benjamin Walker, wit. Mar Set 5: 496-
498

Fabian, James of Parish of St. Bartholomew, Colleton
District, & Margaret Youngblood, decd. (marriage late-
ly solemnized), widow of Peter E. Youngblood, and
granddaughter of Catherine Leitch decd., 30 June 1815;
William Oswald, Alfred Walton, trustees; John Fabian
Senr, Dens. O'Driscol, wit. Mar Set 7: 120-122

Farr, John Dalton C. & Mrs. Lydia Pritchard, of Charleston, 8 Nov 1816; Sanders Glover, John Vinyard, trustees; Mary Jenkins, James Kennedy, wit. Mar Set 7:
126-128

Farr, Nathaniel of St. Pauls Parish, planter, & Kather-
ine Blacklock of Charleston, 13 Nov 1813; William
Blacklock, William Robertson, trustees; James D.
Sommers, Richd. G. Waring, wit. Mar Set 6: 272-277

Fasbender, Dilliman, late of Germany, now of Dist. of
Charleston, & Catherine Gross, widow, 29 April 1803;
Frederick Dubbert, trustee; Chrs. Gradick, Isaac
Nelson, John Geddes, wit. Mar Set 4: 296-301

Fawns, Alexander of St. Peter's Parish, & Lydia C. Pepper
of same, 19 Jan 1815; John Cooper of Purysburg, Alexander S. C. Shaw, trustees; Thos Hardee, Nathl. T.
Patterson, wit. Mar Set 6: 372-374

Fay, Thomas Crittenden, printer & bookseller, of Charleston, & Miss Mary Madeline Broadrick, of Georgetown,
31 Dec 1818; William W. Trapier, trustee; John L.
Wilson, wit. Mar Set 8: 2-3

Fay, Thomas C. & Mary Broderick, 31 Dec 1818, at Georgetown. Pr Geo Winyaw

Fayolle, Theodore Belony & Adele Henlan, 31 Oct 1820.
St Mary's RC

Feay, Obadiah M. of Georgetown Dist., & Esther Woodward,
of Georgetown, widow, 7 Dec 1810; Isaac Course,
Anthony Toomer, trustees; Samuel Smith, John Grant,
wit. Mar Set 6: 16-20

Felix, slave of Mrs. M. Seymour, & Rose, slave of Mrs.
M. Monroe, 5 Sept 1818 in Charleston. St Phil PR

Fell, William of St. Thomas, planter, & Elizabeth Skrine,
of Charleston, spinster, 3 May 1809. Chaston ML

Feraud, Thomas of Charleston, & Elizabeth Casolot of
same, 12 Feb 1819; Charles Lacoste, trustee, Aug.
Poujaud, John Michel, wit. Mar Set 8: 20-23

Ferguson, Barkley of Prince Williams Parish, Beaufort
Dist., planter & Ann McCulloch, widow, & relict of
William McCulloch, decd., 9 April 1803; James Henry
Bowler & Thomas Miller, trustees; Sophia Ferguson,
Benjn Hoagain, Ann Compton, wit. Mar Set 5: 547-549

Ferguson, James B. & Eleanor Dewitt, to Rev. Joshua Lewis,
3 Nov 1809. Marlboro ML

Ffirth, Stubbins of St. Paul's Parish, & Mary Hutchinson,
of St. George Dorchester Parish, daughter of Mathias
Hutchinson, decd., 2 Feb 1814; Joseph Hall Waring,
trustee; Francis Dickinson, Richd. G. Waring, Jos.
Ioor Waring, wit. Mar Set 6: 305-313

Fiche, Peter and Mrs. Ann Proctor, 21 March 1819 in
Charleston. St Phil PR

Figareau & Julie, servants of Mrs. Benoit, 24 Aug 1816.
St Mary's RC

Fillette, Francois & Augustine Brunson Dupont, 6 Feb 1816.
St Mary's RC

Finkley, Thomas G. & Tabitha Ann Stewart, 17 Oct 1819 by
Whitman C. Hill. Georgetown Meth Ch

Finley, Thomas & Jane Clark, 20 Dec 1808. Moses Waddel

Firth, Stebbins, M. D., & Mary Hutchinson, 2 Feb 1814,
in Charleston. St Phil PR

Fischer, John & Louisa Howard, 12 Nov 1816. St Mary's RC

Fitch, Joseph and Miss Caroline H. Bentham, 27 March 1817
in Charleston. St Phil PR

Fitzgerald, John & Deborah Whirskely, 24 June 1817. St
   Mary's RC

Flack, William of St. Paul's Parish, planter, & Julia
   Gallagher, of Charleston, spinster, 22 May 1817; li-
   cense to Revd. Dr. Simon Felix Gallagher. Chaston
   Pro J

Flack, William & Julia Gallagher, 22 May 1817. St Mary's
   RC

Flemming, Thomas & Clarissa Walton, 12 May 1814. 2d Pres
   Ch

Flinn, Rev. Andrew of Charleston & Mrs. Eliza B. Grimball,
   4 March 1811; Revd. William Hollinshead, Morton Waring,
   trustees; Ann H. Darrell, Jane H. McCulla, wit.   Mar
   Set 6: 33-34

Flinn, Rev. Dr. Andrew of Charleston, & wife Eliza B.
   Flinn, late widow of John Grimball, and formerly
   Elizabeth Berkley, daughter of John Berkley, of St.
   Paul's Parish, planter, 6 Feb 1819; Martin Waring,
   trustee; Jacob Ford, Henry Alexander DeSaussure, wit.
   Mar Set 7: 345-354

Floyd, Shadrach & Ann Williams, 18 March 1820. Bryan
   Journal

Fogel, Daniel & Elisabeth Snider, 21 Dec 1810. St Matthews Luth Ch

Fogel, John & Magdelen Houser, 21 Aug 1803. St Matthews
   Luth Ch

Folker, John-Hinds, of Charleston, merchant, & Eliza
   Lloyd, of Charleston, spinster, to Rev. James D.
   Simons, 11 May 1811. Chaston ML

Folker, Thomas of Charleston, druggist, & Esther Lloyd of
   Charleston, spinster, to Rev. James D. Simons, 24 Dec
   1810. Chaston ML

Fooshe, Charles, & Gracy Wood, both of Abbeville Dist.,
   13 June 1820; Elihu Creswell, William Ward, Elizabeth
   M. Ward, wit.   Misc Rec D, pp. 201-202

Foot, Peter D. of New York, and Catharine L. A. Lafar of
   Charleston, 16 Feb 1820; John J. Lafar, trustee; Wm
   Moer, Thomas J. Hands, wit.   Mar Set 8: 97-99

Ford, Joseph S. Dr., of St. Bartholomre's Parish & Mary
   D. Burnet, spinster, 3 March 1819; Henry A. DeSaussure,
   James M. Ford, trustees; Mary M. Elliott, John D.
   Edwards, wit.   Mar Set 8: 14-20

Ford, Stephen & Helen Maria Walter, 24 April 1816; Thomas
Ford, trustee; Sarah James, Sarah Ford, wit. Mar Set
7: 54-55

Ford, Stephen & Hellin Walter, 25 April 1816 on Black
River, 6 miles from Georgetown. Pr Geo Winyaw

Ford, Timothy, of Charleston, attorney, & Mary Magdalene
Prioleau, of the same place, spinster, 20 Nov 1800.
St Phil PR

Forman, William and Betsy Owen, 10 Dec 1801, Hezekiah
Daniel & John Owen, sureties, married by Alexander
Moore, Esq., at the house of John Owen. York Pro
66/3126

Forrcy, Ezekiel & Eliza Clarkson, spinster, 24 April 1811;
Joseph Goultier, trustee, all of Charleston; J. C.
Moses, Thos Harper, Chr. McDonnald, wit. Mar Set 6:
34-37

Foster, James & Mary Davis, 17 June 1806. Moses Waddel

Foures, Jean Antoine & Margaret Boid, 15 Aug 1820. St
Mary's RC

Fournier, Solomon & Marie Francoise Desire, 20 Jan 1813.
St Mary's RC

Fowler, Stanhope & Kezia Laurens, 2 Nov 1815, in Charleston. St Phil PR

Fox, James and Mary Heape, (already married), 11 June
1806; Henry Heape, trustee; Elizabeth Zahler, Jacob
Zahler, wit. Mar Set 5: 220-221

Fox, Patrick of Charleston, & Ann Fleming, 7 Sept 1816;
Jno Russell, Jno Phillips White, wit. Mar Set 7:
155-158

Fox, Patrick & Anne Fleming, 9 Sept 1816. St Mary's RC

Foxley, John W. & Mrs. Margaret Taylor, 2 March 1820 in
Charleston. St Phil PR

Frampton, William of Prince Williams Parish, & Eliza S.
Hughes, of St. Bartholomew's Parish, spinster, 25
Feb 1818; John L. Hunter, Arthur Hughes, trustees;
John Franklin Jr., B. Ferguson, wit. Mar Set 7:
240-243

Francis, Jacques & Marie Faupaint, 1 Aug 1820. St Mary's
RC

Francklow, John Hepworth, & Mary Smith, 6 June 1811. St Matthews Luth Ch

Frampton, William & Miss Violetta Lingard Wyatt, 10 March 1813, in Charleston. St Phil PR

Frank & Venus, slaves of Dr. J. E. Poyas, 6 Nov 1813, in Charleston. St Phil PR

Fraser, Benjamin T. & Agnes Kirkpatrick of Georgetown District, 27 May 1819; Davison McDowall, Robert A. Taylor, trustees; Charlotte Ann Allston, Mary Pyatt Allsont, wit. Mar Set 8: 41-43

Fraser, George & Maria Boone, spinster, of Charleston, 4 May 1809; Thomas Boone, trustee; Jno White, Mary S. Boone, wit. Mar Set 5: 460-466

Fraser, Thomas Loughton Smith & Isabella Wakefield, 1 May 1816 at Charleston. Pr Geo Winyaw

Frazzar, Joh & Betsy Wright, __ Aug 1809; Thomas Mercer, sec. Darl MB

Frean, Gul & Anne Cecelia Haus, 2 March 1813. St Mary's RC

Frean, William & Ann Eliza Hawes, daughter of Mary Hawes, 12 Feb 1813; Henry Gleize, Nathaniel Hawes, trustees; Wm. Hall, E. Pierce, wit. Mar Set 6: 178-181

Freeman, Fleming & Martha Bibb, 16 April 1812. Moses Waddel

Freer, Daniel & Mary Weston, spinster, 16 Jan 1801; Richard Muncreeff, of Wadmalaw Island, trustee; James Bowie, Francis Fickling, Saml Trunker, wit. Mar Set 4: 323-325

Frierson, James, attorney at law & Susan G. Stoll of St. Luke's Parish, 26 Jan 1813; Susan G. Bourquin, trustee; George J. Logan, Geo. Allen, wit. Mar Set 6: 184-186

Frierson, John of St. Mathews Parish, & Eliza Witten, daughter of Peter Witten, decd of St. John's Parish, 11 Dec 1804; James M. Campbell of St. Mathews Parish, & Peter Robert Witten of St. John's Parish, trustees; Peter Witten, Sims Brown, wit. Mar Set 5: 1-2

Froelich, John & Leah Strohman, 10 March 1801. St Matthews Luth Ch

Frost, Thomas The Revd., assistant minister of St. Philip's church, & Miss Anne R. Grimke, 16 June 1818 in Charleston. St Phil PR

Fry, Jacob & Miss Catherine Blewer, 8 Jan 1815 in Charleston. St Phil PR

Fuller, Thomas & Phoebe Louisa Waight, 13 Dec 1812. St Hel PR

Gabbeux, James, of Charleston, and Dorotha Smith, of the same place, spinster, 23 Dec 1802. St Phil PR

Gadsden, Rev. Christopher Edwards, rector of St. Philip's Church, Charleston, & Eliza Allston Bowman, 5 Oct 1816; Esther Lynch, John Gadsden, trustees; James Hamilton, Hugh P. Dawes, wit. Mar Set 7: 73-74

Gadsden, John & Ann M. Edwards, 28 April 1818; James F. Edwards, trustee; E. H. Edwards, J. E. Holmes, wit. Mar Set 7: 249-250

Gadsden, John & Miss Ann Edwards, 29 April 1818 in Charleston. St Phil PR

Gaillard, Bartholomew Esq., merchant & Miss Rebecca C. Doughty, spinster, 6 March 1801. St Phil PR

Gaillard, Bartholomew & Sarah Dounour, 4 Nov 1813 in Charleston. St Phil PR

Gaillard, Charles Junr of St. James Parish, Santee, planter, & Sarah Laborn, widow, 27 Feb 1806; John Shackelford of Georgetown, trustee; Jer. Cuttino, Robt. F. Withers, wit. Mar Set 5: 149-152

Gaillard, Edwin of St. Stephens Parish, physician & wife Mary Harriet Cantey, only daughter of Christopher Gadsden White, decd., 8 June 1820; Samuel Porcher of St. Stephens Parish, planter, trustee. Mar Set 8: 216-218

Gaillard, James, of St. Stephen, planter, & Harriet Porcher, of St. Stephen, spinster, to Rev. Nathl. Bowen, 5 Jan 1810. Chaston ML

Gaillard, Peter the elder, late of St. Stephen's Parish, now of St. John's Parish, Berkley Co., planter & Ann Stevens, widow, 7 Nov 1805; John Palmer Jr. & Joseph Palmer Jr., trustees; Peter Gaillard Jr., Maham Palmer, wit. Mar Set 5: 95-98

Gaillard, Samuel & Mrs. Rinah Jennerett (col'd persons), 19 Dec 1811, in St. Philip's Parish. St Phil PR

Gallevant, James & Mary L. Ranny, 21 April 1814. Bryan
    Journal

Galloway, William, & Mary McPherson, of Marlboro, to Rev.
    Robert Purnell, 30 Aug 1804. Marlboro ML

Gamage, Edward & Mrs. Sarah Simons, 20 March 1817 in
    Charleston. St Phil PR

Gamage, Edward of Charleston Dist., merchant & Sarah
    Simons, widow, daughter of Thomas Barksdale Esqr., late
    of Christ Church Parish, 18 March 1817; George Edwards
    of Beaufort Dist., Thomas Barksdale, brother of said
    Sarah, trustees; John W. Payne, Thos Barksdale, wit.
    Mar Set 7: 139-143

Gannen, Marshall & Sarah Dill, 7 June 1811. St Mary's RC

Garner, Jeremiah, of Charleston, free Negro, & Sarah
    Walker, of Charleston, free Negro, 7 June 1808, to
    Rev. George Buist. Chaston ML

Gadsden, Christopher, of Charleston, Esquire, & Mary-
    Sidney Ash, of Charleston, spinster, 20 Feb 1810.
    Chaston ML

Gany, slave of Mr. I. D. Tough & Catherine Kinloch, free
    person of color, 9 June 1819 in Charleston. St Phil PR

Garden, Alexander Wigfall of Clarendon County, doctor of
    physic, & Sarah Johnson, daughter of Thomas Nightin-
    gale Johnson, decd., 20 May 1818; Louisa J. Schroder,
    wit. Mar Set 7: 271-274

Garden, Alexander W. & Miss Anna Maria Brailsford, 7 May
    1818 in Charleston. St Phil PR

Garick, George & Margaret Brandeburg, 3 Oct 1809. St
    Matthews Luth Ch

Garick, Jacob & Magdelen Brandeburg, 12 May 1811. St
    Matthews Luth Ch

Garick, John & Catherine Fogel, 12 May 1801. St Matthews
    Luth Ch

Garick, William & Anne Snider, 24 July 1810. St Matthews
    Luth Ch

Garlington, Edwin & Eleamor Griffin, Laurens Dist., 23
    Nov 1815; John Cook, Elihu Creswell, wit.   Misc Rec C
    pp. 231-233

Gates, Christian & Magdelen Switzer, 8 Feb 1810. St
    Matthews Luth Ch

Gates, Frederick & Rosina Irick, 12 Jan 1807. St Matthews Luth Ch

Gaulden, Wade H. & Ann Chivers, of Sumter Dist., 25 Nov 1816; Benjn G. Ioor, trustee, Thomas Eveleigh, wit. Misc Rec C, pp. 392-394

Gaunt, Nebo, son of Zebulon Gaunt, decd., Newberry Dist., S. C., & Judith Wright, 29 Apr 1802. Bush R MM

Gaunt, Samuel, Newberry Dist., S. C., & Susanna Julien, 11 July 1807. Bush R MM

Gause, Benjamin of Horry District, planter, & Elizabeth Senter, of Dist. of Georgetown, 26 Dec 1820; Isaac Carr of Dist. of Georgetown, trustee; Margaret Croft, Sarah Tamplet, wit. Mar Set 8: 207-209

George, slave of Mrs. Roger Pinckney & Juno Simons (free colored person), both baptized persons, 29 Oct 1812. St Phil PR

Gerald, Benjamin of Sumter Dist., & Alice James of same, brother of Samuel James, 26 June 1802; Ann Howard, Wm Bay, wit. Misc Rec B, pp. 194-195

Gerald, Samuel Sr. of Horry Dist., & wife Zilpha, 28 Oct 1819; Hardy Lewis, trustee; Samuel Floyd, Bethel Gerreld, wit. Horry DB B-1, pp. 176-177

Gervais, Paul T. Revd. & Miss Claudia G. Thayer, 1 Jan 1819. St Phil PR

Geyer, John of Charleston, gent., & Mary Oakford, widow, __ Jan 1810; Alexander H. McGillivray, vendue master, trustee; Thos Bampfield, J. Bampfield, Rebecca Screven, wit. Mar Set 5: 511-513

Gibbes, Allston & Sarah Maxwell Chisolm, 31 Dec 1818 in Charleston. St Phil PR

Gibbes, George Morgan, of Charleston, planter, & Eliza Gardenia Garden of Charleston, spinster, 26 Nov 1813; license to Right Rev. Theodore Dehon. Chaston Pro J

Gibbes, Rev. Henry of Waccamaw, & Miss Ann Isabella Mayrant, 15 May 1820. Holy Cross Ch

Gibbes, James L. of Charleston & Adelaide G. Elliott, daughter of Mrs. Juliet G. Elliott, 28 Jan 1817; Wilmot S. Gibbes, of Chester Dist., trustee; Robert Gibbes, Jr., John Reeve Gibbes, wit. Mar Set 7: 134-139

Gibbes, John Walter, son of John Walter Gibbes, decd., &
Mary Charlotte Mayer, sister of John G. Mayer, and
Jacob R. Mayer, Charleston, 2 Nov 1814; Ann Wyatt,
Christopher Nelson, wit.   Mar Set 6: 383-386

Gibbes, Joseph Smith of Charleston & Amelia Shoolbred,
daughter of James Shoolbred, and his deceased wife
Mary, daughter of Thomas Middleton, 11 May 1816; John
Gibbes, Robert Reeves Gibbes Jr., trustees; Charles
Drayton Jr., wit.   Mar Set 7: 49-54

Gibbes, Joseph Smith of Charleston, planter, & Amelia
Sarah Shoolbred, of Charleston, spinster, 11 May 1816;
license to Rev. Dr. William Percy. Chaston Pro J

Gibbes, Lewis-Ladson, of Charleston, Esquire, & Maria-
Henrietta Drayton, of St. Andrew, spinster, to Rev.
Thomas Mills, 19 July 1809. Chaston ML

Gibbes, Robert & Miss Sarah Gibbes, 28 Nov 1816 in Charleston. St Phil PR

Gibbes, Wilmot S. Esq. & Miss Anna Frances DeSaussure,
10 Dec 1805; Henry William DeSaussure, trustee; John
D. Rivers, Jacob Ford, wit.   Mar Set 5: 98-100

Gibert, Joseph Dr. & Jane Terry, 24 Jan 1815. Moses
Waddel

Gibert, Stephen & Sarah Pettigrew, 4 June 1804. Moses
Waddel

Gibson, Alexander of Charleston, merchant, & Elizabeth
Ewing, daughter of Adam Ewing, decd., 15 May 1815;
John S. Peake, Alexander Sinclair, trustees; Mary
Moore, Archd. S. Johnston, wit.   Mar Set 6: 378-381

Gibson, Capt. John & Miss Martha Savage, 6 Sept 1809;
Thos Godbold Esq., sec.   Marion ML

Gilbert, David & Catherine Piegler, 31 Dec 1807. St
Matthews Luth Ch

Gilbert, John L. & Jane Moragne, 16 May 1810. Moses
Waddel

Gilchrist, Adam of Charleston, & Elizabeth Lamboll Thomas, 3 Feb 1812; Joseph Dulles, Paul T. Jones, trustees; Josiah Taylor, John Woddrop, wit.   Mar Set 6:
96-100

Gilchrist, Adam of Charleston, Esquire, & Elizabeth-Lam-
boll Thomas, of Charleston, spinster, to Rev. Isaac
L. Keith, 4 Feb 1812. Chaston ML

Gilchrist, Edmund & Nancy Thomson , 8 Sept 1818. Moses Waddel

Giles, Abraham of Marion District, planter & Annes Phillips, of same, spinster, 16 Feb 1804; Philip Phillips, Isaac Phillips, trustees; John Phillips, James Ervin, wit. Mar Set 4: 416-420

Giles, Abraham & Anne Phillips, both of Marion Dist., 16 Feb 1804; Philip Phillips & Isaac Phillips, trustees; John Phillips, James Ervin, wit. Misc Rec B, pp. 295-300

Giles, Andrew & Sarah Patterson, 5 March 1812. Moses Waddel

Giles, Othniel John of Charleston, & Rebecca Perry, spinster, daughter of Joseph Perry, late of St. Pauls Parish, decd., 4 March 1806; Col. James Postell, of St Luke's Parish, trustee; Charles Pelot, James Postell Junr., wit. Mar Set 5: 193-197

Gillespie, Mathew & Rachel Ward, 18 Feb 1808. Moses Waddel

Gillman, _____ & Mrs. Ann Kershaw, widow of George Kershaw, born Ann Hutchins, 7 May 1812. Kershaw Diary

Gillon, Alexander, factor & Sarah H. Brisbane, daughter of John Brisbane, 16 Dec 1816; William Henry Parker, trustee; Edwin C. Holland, Jno M. Ogier, wit. Mar Set 7: 96-100

Gilman, George, late of Camden now of Black River, planter, & Ann Kershaw, widow of George Kershaw decd. of Camden, 27 Apr 1812; James Brown, Benjamin Bineham, Richard Lloyd Champion of Camden, trustees; Joseph Thornton, Samuel Brown, wit. Misc Rec B, pp. 736-738

Gilman, Tadock & Miss Elizabeth Beedum, 1 May 1816 in St. Philip's Church. St Phil PR

Girardeau, Peter Bohun and Miss Maria Pinckney, 15 May 1817 in St. Bartholomew's. St Phil PR

Giraud, Francois & Adelaide Fayolle, 4 March 1817. St Mary's RC

Gist, States of St. Andrews Parish, planter, & Sarah Brandford Porcher, of St. Pauls Parish, spinster, __ Dec 1814; Thomas Wright Bacot, Henry Harramond Bacot, trustees; Robert M. Hay, Susan S. May, wit. Mar Set 6: 417-419

Gleize, Dr. Henry Etienne & Susannah Peigne, otherwise
known as Susannah Vallaneuve, 12 Nov 1808; James
Miller, trustee, all of Charleston; Alexr Christie, J.
Fowler, John S. Cogdell, wit.   Mar Set 5: 413-417

Glisson, John W. & wife Sarah, of New Port, Rhode Island,
11 June 1817; Charles E. Rowand of Charleston, trustee; Edwin C. Holland, wit.   Mar Set 7: 183-185

Glover, Joseph of Charleston, Doctor of Medicine and wife
Elizabeth Slann, Glover, 24 Aug 1805; Edward Darrell
Smith, M. D., trustee; Daniel D'Oyley Jr., James Dun-
can, wit.   Mar Set 5: 67-63

Glover, William & Lucy Reeves, 5 Nov 1804, Willis Reeves,
surety.   York Pro 66/3134

Godber, William of Charleston & Martha Hinson of same,
21 Feb 1805; Simeon Theus, James Blair, trustees; W.
B. Minott, Benjn Minott, wit.   Mar Set 5: 39-44

Godbold, Hugh G. & Rhody Crawford, 24 Sept 1817. Marion
ML

Godefrey, Aemand, and Mrs. Maria Spencer, 15 April 1820
in Charleston. St Phil PR

Godfrey, John of St. Bartholomew's Parish, attorney at
law, & Eliza Webb Ladson Webb, 28 March 1818; Peter
B. Girardeau, William C. Pinckney, trustees; Geo
Taylor, Susan P. Webb, wit.   Mar Set 7: 250-253

Gondrand, Antoine, ship carpenter, of Charleston & Elizabeth Boillat, widow, 6 Nov 1802; John B. Logan, John
E. Cardind, trustees; Francis Cornie, wit.   Mar Set
4: 229-230

Good, John & Susannah Connell, 6 March 1816; Timothy
Dargan, trustee, Darlington Dist., Wm F. Zimmerman,
A. B. Woods, Jas Woods, wit.   Misc Rec C, pp. 281-
283

Goode, Samuel W. & Eliza Hamilton, __ Jan 1800. Moses
Waddel

Goodman, Jacob & Sarah Baker, 12 Jan 1810. Moses Waddel

Gordon, Charles P. & Miss Margaret E. Campbell, 5 July
1817 in St. Philip's Church. St Phil PR

Gordon, James & Teresa Roberts, col'd persons, 2 Feb 1814
in Charleston. St Phil PR

Gordon, John of Charleston & Mrs. Catharine Freeman, 23 May 1816; Isom Lowry, trustee; Tho. Cordray, Loammi Baker, wit.   Mar Set 7: 55-56

Gordon, John & Jane M. Buris, 19 Nov 1818 at Williamsburgh.   Pr Geo Winyaw

Gough, Richard & Mary Parker, free persons of color, 20 Jan 1819 in Charleston.   St Phil PR

Gough, Richard Sydney & Rachel Nevarro Sarah Dunning, 17 Feb 1814, in Charleston.   St Phil PR

Gould, George & Nancy Posey, 11 Aug 1808.   Moses Waddel

Graddick, Richard & Sarah Sweeny, 17 Dec 1818.   2d Pres Ch

Graham, Prince & Sarah James, free persons of color, 7 April 1819 in Charleston.

Graham, Thomas & Margaret Corre, 5 Jan 1813; James Douglas, Lewis Monnar, trustees; all of Charleston; Jacob F. Mintzing, A. Devillers, wit.   Mar Set 6: 257-261

Gramner, Jacob & Nancy Dent, 13 April 1820.   Drehr Journal

Grant, Henry & Mary Lewis, free persons of color, 9 March 1818 in Charleston.   St Phil PR

Grant, Stephen & Eliza. Graves, 5 May 1805.   Bryan Journal

Graves, Peter & Sarah Tann, 15 Sept 1801.   Bryan Journal

Graves, Richard Esqr., adminral of the Navy of his Britannic Majesty, now residing at Brussels, Netherlands, & Louisa Caroline Graves, his wife, now residing at Idsworth Park, Hants County, England, daughter of Sir John Colleton, late of Exeter County of Devon, England, decd., 17 June 1817; Tristram Radcliffe, C. J. Hector, wit.   Mar Set 7: 260-265

Graves, Samuel Colleton of S. C., & Susan McPherson, daughter of Gen. John McPherson, decd., of Charleston, 15 April 1818; James E. McPherson, guardian of Susan; James R. Pringle, James McPherson Jr., trustees; Wm Robertson, Robert Pringle, wit.   Mar Set 7: 243-249

Gray, Arthur & Polly Adams, 30 March 1815.   Moses Waddel

Gray, Daniel Rev. & Mary Hutton, __ April 1803. Moses Waddel

Gray, James & Elizabeth Roberts, 3 May 1814.   Moses Waddel

Gray, John & Elizabeth Petigru, 21 Feb 1805.   Moses Waddel

Gray, William & Mary Weed, 14 May 1818.   Moses Waddel

Grayson, John of Charleston, mariner, & Frances Anne
  Harvey, of Charleston, spinster, 17 Sept 1816; license
  to Christopher Edwards Gadsden.   Chaston Pro J

Grayson, John & Frances Ann Harvey, 17 Sept 1816 in
  Charleston.   St Phil PR

Grayson, William John of Beaufort, & Sarah Matilda Somarsall, granddaughter of Daniel Stevens of Charleston,
  5 Jan 1814; William H. Joyner, wit.   Mar Set 6: 293-
  294

Green, Christopher Rhodes & Mary Ann Lehre, daughter of
  Ann Lehre, 26 Dec 1815; Charles W. Doyley, trustee;
  Luke Reed, A. J. Browne, wit.   Mar Set 7: 1-6

Green, James & Sarah Wilson, both of our Society, __ May
  1814.   Georgetown Meth Ch

Green, John Thompson Jun. & Miss Elizabeth Blackwell of
  Williamsburgh District, __ July 1813 by Joseph Travis.
  Georgetown Meth Ch

Green, Peter-Archor of York District, gentleman, & Sarah
  Walton, of Charleston, spinster, to Rev. Richd. Furman,
  1 March 1809.   Chaston ML

Greene, Christopher R. & Miss Mary Lehre, 26 Dec 1815 in
  Charleston.   St Phil PR

Greet, James of Charleston, mariner, & Jane Allen, of
  the same place, 12 April 1801.   St Phil PR

Gregg, Robert, Esquire, & Mary Ann McIlveen, spinster,
  26 Feb 1807.   Marion ML

Gregorie, James, merchant in Charleston, and Miss Ann
  Ladson, of the same place, spinster, 3 Feb 1801.   St
  Phil PR

Greile, Claude & wife Caroline Pennetier Greille, ___
  1815; Mme. Muirel Pennetier, trustee; J. Bayol, C.
  Tesson, wit. (original in French).   Mar Set 7: 37-40

Grey, John & Mrs. Bridget Jones, 15 Oct 1816 in Charleston.   St Phil PR

Grice, Wm. H. & Mary Foxworth, 6 May 1806.   Marion ML

Griffin, Clinton of Kentucky & Sarah Smith, of Charleston, 8 Aug 1811; John Roche, trustee; Richd Wall, Thos Fowle, wit. Mar Set 6: 55-56

Grille, Claude & Caroline Pennetier, 22 Sept 1814. St Mary's RC

Grimball, Paul Jr. of Charleston, gentleman, & Elizabeth Hanscome of Johns Island, widow, 4 June 1814; Benjamin Jenkins of Wadmalaw Island, trustee; John Townsend, Saml Jenkins, wit. Mar Set 6: 333-337

Grimke, John & Miss Sophia Ladson, 23 April 1816 in Charleston. St Phil PR

Gruber, John of Colleton Dist., planter & Ann Rumph Koger, of same, spinster, 9 June 1817; Joseph Koger Jr., trustee; John Koger, Maria E. Koger, Danl. R. Sullivan, wit. Mar Set 7: 185-186

Guerard, Jacob Esqr., of Beaufort Dist., & Ann Fraser, of Charleston, spinster, 23 June 1820; Charles Fraser, brother of Ann, trustee; Augustus Winthrop, Charles Winthrop, wit. Mar Set 8: 147-150

Guerard, John of St. Luke's Parish, & Sophia Percy of Charleston, spinster, 26 Dec 1809; James Legare, Barnard Elliott Bee, trustees; Wm Boyd, James Sanders, wit. Mar Set 5: 502-508

Guerard, John of St. Luke, planter, & Sophia Percy, of Charleston, spinster, to Rev. William Percy, 26 Dec 1809. Chaston ML

Guerin, Robert, of Charleston-Neck, farmer, & Mary Ellis, of Charleston, widow, to Rev. Richard Furman, 19 Feb 1810. Chaston ML

Guibert, Louis & Jeanne Fanse, 20 Feb 1815. St Mary's RC

Guilvery, Jean Baptiste & Maria Calhoun, 29 July 1816. St Mary's RC

Gurfin, John & Mrs. Mary Ann White, 25 Dec 1815 in Charleston. St Phil PR

Guy, servant of Mr. S. Smith & Amey, of Mrs. C. Allston, 28 Dec 1817, at Georgetown. Pr Geo Winyaw

Gwynn, Leonard & Polly Payne, 12 Dec 1811. Moses Waddel

Habersham, John, now in the town of Beaufort, & Ann Barnwell, spinster, 8 Jan 1812; John Gibbes Barnwell, Robert Barnwell, trustees; James E. B. Finley, R. Means, Sarah Barnwell, wit. Mar Set 6: 117-121

Habersham, Wm & Miss Maria B. Elliott, 15 Feb 1816, in Charleston. St Phil PR

Haig, James & Elizabeth Purcell (colored), 20 July 1814, in Charleston. St Phil PR

Haig, Maham of St. Johns Parish, physician, & Elizabeth Motee of Charleston, spinster, 22 July 1820; Maurice Simons, factor, trustee; Charlotte Broughton, Mary J. Motte, Keatg. Simons, wit. Mar Set 8: 156-160

Haigler, Henry & Miss Mary Catherine Gates, 22 Nov 1800. St Matthews Luth Ch

Hair, James & Margaret Snider, 5 Aug 1802. St Matthews Luth Ch

Hale, Samuel, of the State of North Carolina, & Margaret Gregg of Jefferies Creek, 31 Jan 1803; license directed to Rev. James Hale. Marion ML

Hall, Thomas, of Charleston, bricklayer, and Sarah Howard, of the same place, spinster, 20 July 1802. St Phil PR

Hall, William Dr. & Miss Ann Poyas, 9 May 1815 in Charleston. St Phil PR

Hallonquist, D. D., from London & Marian Hatton, 17 Dec 1812. St Hel PR

Halsall, John Eberley of Charleston, butcher, & Elizabeth Venter, of Charleston, spinster, 24 Dec 1819; license to Revd. John Bachman. Chaston Pro J

Hamer, William & Unicey Curganey, to Rev. Wm. Bennett, 25 July 1811. Marlboro ML

Hamilton, Archibald & Jane Davis, 17 Dec 1807. Moses Waddel

Hamilton, John & Miss Mary Pritchard, 26 Dec 1811 in St. Philip's Parish. St Phil PR

Hamlin, John & Miss Ann Dewees, 13 Jan 1820 in Mazyckborough. St Phil PR

Hamlin, Thomas of Charleston, school-master, & Emily Edgeworth, of Charleston, spinster, 24 June 1809. Chaston ML

Hammond, slave of Mr. J. S. Dart & Sarah, slave of Miss R. Russell, 3 Dec 1818 in Charleston. St Phil PR

Hammond, Samuel of the State of Georgia, Esqr., Eliza
Amelia O'Keefe, single woman of Barnwell Dist., 25 May
1802; Dickie Garlington, William Williamson, wit.
Misc Rec B, pp. 176-180

Hampton, Wade Junr. & Miss Ann Fitzsimons, 6 March 1817
in Charleston. St Phil PR

Handey, Thomas of Charleston & Catharine Barre, widow,
5 April 1802; James McTeer, coachmaker, of Charleston,
trustee; W. H. Torrans, Danl. U. Turner, wit. Mar
Set 4: 164-168

Hanly, Philip, of Ninagh, County of Tipperary, merchant,
& Mary Carroll of Toomavara, same county, spinster;
Honora Carroll of Toomavara, trustee, brother of sd.
Mary; James Parsons of Charleston, S. C., decd., uncle
of sd. Mary Carroll; Dl. Murphy, J. P. Kennedy, wit.
7 Sept 1813. Mar Set 8: 6-9

Harbers, John Ramdolph & Olivete Colman, 13 Jan 1818.
St Mary's RC

Harbuck, John & Sally Rogers, 21 Feb 1811. Moses Waddel

Hardwick, James & Miss Mary Susan Miloina Serine, 13 Nov
1817, by William Capers. Georgetown Meth Ch

Hardwick, Richard & Margeret Roy, 22 April 1804. St
Matthews Luth Ch

Hargreaves, Joseph of Charleston, merchant, & Elizabeth
Blandford Cantey, widow of James Cantey, of Liberty
Co., Georgia, 9 Jan 1801; William Inglesby, Joshua
Hargreaves, trustees; William Veree, Joseph Peace,
wit. Mar Set 4: 41-45

Harleston, Edward Junr & Miss Georgianna Doughty, 2
March 1818 in Charleston. St Phil PR

Harleston, John of City of Charleston, & Elizabeth Cades,
daughter of Thomas Cades, Esqr., decd., ____ 1819;
James Cades, trustee; Robert Little, Jas. Mathews,
wit. Mar Set 8: 38-41

Harman, Jacob & Elizabeth Wise, 21 Sept 1819. Drehr
Journal

Harman, Jacob & Barbara Stingley, 6 July 1820. Drehr
Journal

Harper, John & Eliza. Ramsey, 11 May 1802. Bryan Journal

Harper, John, & Jane Currey, his second wife, 6 March
1806. Bryan Journal

Harrell, Lewis & Miss Elizabeth Holloway, license dated
   24 Dec 1813; married 18 Jan 1814, by Daniel Smith,
   V. D. M. Darl MB

Harrington, James, & Eleanor Wilson, to Rev. Joshua Lewis,
   17 Dec 1808. Marlboro ML

Harris, Amos & Anne Stoutenmyer, 7 May 1807. St Matthews
   Luth Ch

Harris, James & Mary Clark, 8 Oct 1818. Moses Waddel

Harris, John & Mrs. Ann Hodgkinson, 7 April 1816 in
   Charleston. St Phil PR

Harris, Lud & Eliza Walker, 22 Dec 1803. Moses Waddel

Harris, Nathaniel & Margaret McElvie, 26 July 1810.
   Moses Waddel

Harris, Obadiah, son of Obadiah & Mary Harris, decd.,
   Guilford Co., N. C. & Mary Moorman, daughter of
   Zachariah & Mary Moorman, Marlborough Dist., S. C.,
   25 March 1802. Piney Grove MM

Harris, William & Cynthia Harper, 29 Jan 1811. Moses
   Waddel

Harrison, Ben & Mehetabel Bryan, 6 Feb 1818. Bryan
   Journal

Harrison, James & Mehitable Pillsbury, 6 Feb 1812. 2d
   Pres Ch

Harvey, Edward Trescot & Mrs. Martha Lafilley, 14 Feb
   1820 in Charleston. St Phil PR

Harvick, Nicholas & Nancy King, 23 Nov 1808. Moses
   Waddel

Hasell, Andrew of Charleston, planter, & Hannah-Cochran
   Ash, of Charleston, spinster, 20 Feb 1810. Chaston ML

Hasell, Christopher G. & Miss Matilda Perry, 14 Jan 1811,
   in St. George's Parish. St Phil PR

Hasell, James & Miss Margaret Dawes, 3 April 1805; Alexander Edwards, trustee; John Gadsden, wit. Mar Set
   5: 131-132

Hasell, William Soranzo of Charleston, attorney at law,
   & Elizabeth G. Tart, spinster, 10 July 1806; Dr. Alex-
   ander Garden, William Hasell Gibbs, trustees; John S.
   Cogdell, Henry H. Bacot, wit. Mar Set 5: 316-333

Hasket, Isaac & Rebekah Evans, daughter of Robert Evans decd., Newberry Dist., S. C., 2 Nov 1803. Bush R MM

Haslen, Frederick & Josephene Durbee, 25 Nov 1813 in Charleston. St Phil PR

Haslum, Thomas & Mary Mack, 21 Feb 1804. St Matthews Luth Ch

Haslum, William & Margeret Felder, 31 Dec 1809. St Matthews Luth Ch

Hauck, John of Charleston, & Margaret Wolf, widow of John Frederick Wolf, decd., _____ 1802; David Chalmers, Langdon Cheves, wit. Mar Set 4: 199-204

Hawes, Nathaniel & Mary Frean, 1 Jan 1815. St Mary's RC

Hawes, Oliver, physician, & Mary Bonneau Leigh, of George-town Dist., 1 May 1800; John Cogdell, trustee; Jacob Wm Harvey, Saml Leonard, wit. Mar Set 3, pp. 440-442

Hawkins, Isaac, son of Isaac & Margaret Hawkins, Union Dist., & Mary Cook, daughter of Amos & Elizabeth Cook, 25 March 1802. Cane Cr MM

Hawkins, Isaac, son of Nathan & Ann Hawkins, Union Dist., & Martha Kenworthy, daughter of Joshua & Mary Kenworthy, 27 Jan 1803. Cane Cr MM

Hay, Robert McKewn & Susannah Singleton Porcher, daughter of Peter Porcher Junr., late of St. Peter's Parish, 15 Dec 1809; Thomas Wright Bacot, Joseph Porcher, trustees; Tho. Akin, H. H. Bacot, wit. Mar Set 5: 521-522

Hayes, David of Charleston, store-keeper, & Lydia-Eliza-beth Deliessline, of Charleston, spinster, to Rev. James D. Simons, 21 Dec 1809. Chaston ML

Haynsworth, John of Charleston, merchant, & Mary-Magda-lene-Hortensia Delorme, of Charleston, spinster, 12 Oct 1808. Chaston ML

Hazlehurst, Robert Junr & Elizabeth Pettingale Wilson, daughter of Leighton Wilson (no date, recorded 19 Jan 1818); G. A. Hazlehurst, wit. Mar Set 7: 220-221

Heard, John Esqr. of Barnwell Dist., & Jane Barnard of Edgefield Dist., 13 July 1809; Robert Barnard Senr., George Haupt, wit. Misc Rec B, pp. 589-593

Heath, John D. & Eliza Desel, daughter of Charles Desel, decd., 7 Nov 1808; Henry Muckenfuss, Samuel Desel, trustees; Mary Desel, John Warnock, wit. Mar Set 5: 427-431

Heery, Thomas & Eliza Austin, 20 Oct 1820. St Mary's RC

Heffernan, Joseph & Rosana Gallagher, 19 Nov 1820. St Mary's RC

Hemphill, James & Mary LeRoy, 16 March 1819. Moses Waddel

Henneguin, Jean Baptiste, & Marie Joseph Olman, widow, 9 Sept 1802; Peter Smith, trustee; Leves P. Mooney, Peter Levrier, wit. Mar Set 4: 205-206

Henniguin, John Baptiste, of Charleston, confectioner, and Mary Josepha Olman, of the same place, widow, 9 Sept 1802. St Phil PR

Henning, John & Jane Green Junior, 15 May 1806; Richard Green Jr., trustee; Thomas Henning, Jas. Green, wit. (Georgetown District). Mar Set 5: 261-264

Henry, slave of Mr. Shrewsbury & Grace, slave of Dr. Poyas, 28 Sept 1815 in Charleston. St Phil PR

Henry, Jacob P. of Savannah, Ga., & Frances Maria Myers, eldest daughter of Levy Myers, of Charleston, 28 Nov 1814; Levy Myers, Mordecai Myers, trustees; Jacob Cohen, Jacob Moise, wit. Mar Set 6: 360-366

Herbemont, Nicholas, & Caroline Smyth, Richland Dist., 21 July 1808; Edward Fisher, Abraham Nott, trustees; John Glaze, James S. Giagnard, wit. Misc Rec. H, 482-484

Herd, Benjamin F. & Martha Bowering, 24 Oct 1807; John DeBow, trustee; Sarah Lawrence, wit. Mar Set 5: 345-346

Heriot, Major Benjamin D. and Miss Sophia H. Harris, 8 Feb 1816, in Charleston. St Phil PR

Heriot, Robert of Georgetown, attorney at law, & Sarah Caroline Heriot, spinster, daughter of George Heriot, of Georgetown, merchant, 12 Jan 1802; Roger Heriot, trustee; John Tucker, Leonard White, Eliza Tucker, wit. Mar Set 4: 129-137

Heriot, Robert, of Georgetown & Maria Heriot, 12 June 1804; Robert Brownfield of Georgetown, trustee; C. DuPre, G. W. Heriot, wit. Mar Set 4: 416-420

Herren, Edmond of Pee Dee & Jane Thomas, of same, both of Marion District, 3 Jan 1801; license directed to Rev. Philip Kerton. Marion ML

Herring, William & Beatrix Collier, 14 May 1818. Moses Waddel

Herviant, Pierre Michel & Pibronille Dubarry, 13 April 1812. St Mary's RC

Hevey, James & Frances Sweeney, 16 Jan 1820. St Mary's RC

Hext, James Hartley & Mary Brailsford, 15 June 1812 in Charleston. St Phil PR

Heyward, Thomas of St. Luke's Parish, planter, & Ann E. Cuthbert of Prince William's Parish, spinster, granddaughter of Mary Cuthbert and Ann Heyward, 24 Dec 1812; John Alexander Cuthbert Sr., James Cuthbert, Thomas Cuthbert, John Alexander Cuthbert Jr., & George Wigg Cuthbert of Prince William's Parish, trustees; William Taylor, Daniel D'Oyley, William Martin, wit. Mar Set 6: 205-208

Hickey, Andrew & Mary Cherry, both of Orangeburgh Dist., 26 Dec 1816; Daniel Gissendanner, trustee; Ephram Miller, John Gissendanner, wit. Misc Rec C, pp. 397-398

High, Henry, & Sophia Younginger, 26 April 1814. St Michaels Luth Ch

Highma, Thomas of Charleston, merchant, & Frances-Charlotte Hubert, of Charleston, spinster, to Rev. Nathaniel Bowen, 2 June 1809. Chaston ML

Hillard, Nathaniel-Green, of Charleston, mariner & Ann Watt, of Charleston, spinster, to Rev. Wm. Hollinshead, 7 March 1809. Chaston ML

Hillen, Ebenezer of Georgetown & Mary Dudley, 17 Nov 1808; Francis Kinlock of Georgetown Dist., Esqr., trustee; William Grant, John Grant, wit. Mar Set 6: 127-130

Hillhouse, Joseph & Harriet Gibert, 9 July 1817. Moses Waddel

Hillman, William & Elizabeth Buckeley, 13 Nov 1814. St Mary's RC

Hills, James B. Dr., & Miss Mary Wyatt, 30 Nov 1815 in Charleston. St Phil PR

Hinds, James & Ann Scanlan, 22 Jan 1820. St Mary's RC

Hinson, Lazarus, & Sarah Harvel, to Rev. Joshua Lewis, 15 Nov 1807. Marlboro ML

Hinton, Robert D. & Eliza D. Prior, 4 Dec 1810; Thomas Gelzer, Charles Hurst, trustees; J. W. Chitty, Thos. Blackmon, wit. Mar Set 6: 4-6

Hiott(?), _____ & Mary Beech, 5 Dec 1811. Bryan Journal

Hiott, Sam. & Martha Beech, 22 March 1810. Bryan Journal

Hobby, William J. & Sarah Williamson, __ Feb 1804. Moses Waddel

Hodge, John of Charleston and wife Ann (late Ann Cotton), 16 Aug 1806; John Rouch of Charleston, trustee; Tho. Fowler, wit. Mar Set 5: 237-243

Hoey, John of Charleston, grocer, & Mary Estes, of Charleston, widow, to Rev. James D. Simons, 1 March 1810. Chaston ML

Hoffman, Jacob & Sophia Zimmerman, 26 Jan 1804. St Matthews Luth Ch

Hoffman, John & Elisabeth Hair, 30 Dec 1801. St Matthews Luth Ch

Holins, Edmon & Mary Joudon, 30 July 1814, by A. Senter. Georgetown Meth Ch

Hollinger, James Jeremiah & Elizabeth Moss, spinster, both of St. Peter's Parish, 13 Dec 1816; Richard Winkler, trustee; James Porcher, Edward Wall, wit. Mar Set 7: 161-162

Hollingsworth, Jacob, son of Joseph decd. & Margaret Hollingsworth, Laurence Co., S. C. & Martha Henderson, daughter of Nathaniel & Rebekah, Edgefield Dist., S. C., 1 Aug 1800. Bush R MM

Holm, Andrew of Charleston, mariner & Ann Middleton, of Charleston, widow, 4 June 1816; license to Rev. Andrew Flyn. Chaston Pro J

Holman, Conrad & Rachell Noble, 2 July 1807. St Matthews Luth Ch

Holman, Joseph & Anna Parler, 18 Dec 1806. St Matthews Luth Ch

Holman, Joseph George & Miss Mary Latimer, 23 Feb 1817 in Charleston. St Phil PR

Holmes, Andrew of Charleston, gentleman, & Margaret Gray of the same place, spinster, 22 May 1800. St Phil PR

Holmes, Edward Isaac & Miss Mary E. Holmes, 4 March 1818 in Charleston. St Phil PR

Holmes, Isaac Legare, of Johns Island, planter & Harriet Air of Charleston, widow, 10 Nov 1810; Henry P. Holmes, trustee; John Ward, George Barksdale, wit. Mar Set 6: 24-26

Holmes, James & Miss Sarah Freer, 8 Nov 1817 in St. Philip's Church. St Phil PR

Holmes, James T. W. of Charleston, & wife Caroline (formerly Caroline Rivers, daughter of Josiah Rivers, of James Island, decd.), 13 May 1817; John W. Holmes, Rawlins Rivers, trustees; Sarah Rivers, John E. Rivers, wit. Mar Set 7: 178-182

Holms, Mabary & Ann Jaudon, both of near this place, 23 July 1815. Georgetown Meth Ch

Holt, Nathaniel of Charleston, soldier, & Anne Cherrytree, of Charleston, widow, 11 Feb 1815; license to Mr. Alexr Talley. Chaston Pro J

Hopkins, Thos & Eliz. English, 2 Feb 1800. Kershaw Diary

Horlbeck, John & Mrs. Maria Lord, 12 Nov 1815 in Charleston. St Phil PR

Horry, Charles Lucas Pinckney, son of Daniel Horry and wife Harriett Pinckney, & Eleonore Maria Florimonde Defay Latourmabourg, daughter of Charles Marie Cesar Defay Latourmabourg and wife Marie Charlotte Henriette Pinault de Tenelles, 30 June 1809. (original in French) Mar Set 6: 48-52

Houck, Casper & Anne Moorer, 25 May 1802. St Matthews Luth Ch

Houseal, David of Charleston, merchant, & Margaret Lilly of same, widow, 3 Aug 1809; John Langton, Ebenezer Hopkins, trustees; Aug. Poujand, Jeremiah Paschal, wit. Mar Set 5: 472-476

Houser, Jacob & Elisabeth Hoffman, 31 Dec 1801. St Matthews Luth Ch

Houston, James R. & Nancy Hughes, 21 May 1818. Moses Waddel

Howard, Alexander & Louise H. Petsch, 27 Oct 1814, in Charleston. St Phil PR

Howard, Richard & Rebecca Jolley of Pee Dee, Marion District, 29 Sept 1800; license directed to Rev. Mr. McCullough. Marion ML

Howard, Richard Francis, of Charleston, cooper, & Eliza Grathan, of the same place, 25 Feb 1802. St Phil PR

Howard, Richard-Francis of Charleston, Cooper, & Elizabeth Washington Mazyck, of Charleston, spinster, to Rev. William Percy, 3 Feb 1812. Chaston ML

Howard, William V. & Hanna Elfe, 20 Oct 1812, in Charleston. St Phil PR

Howland, Benjamin Tucker of Georgetown, mariner, & Elizabeth Morton, 21 May 1808; C. DuPre, wit. Mar Set 5: 479

Howland, Benjamin-Tucker, of Charleston, mariner & Elizabeth Morton, of Charleston, spinster, 21 May 1808. Chaston ML

Howren, Robert of Georgetown Dist., & Martha Young Simmons, of same, 25 Dec 1816; John L. Wilson, Peter Simmons, trustees; Nimrod Howren, Jno Simons, wit. Mar Set 7: 100-101

Howren, Robert & Miss Martha Simons, 24 Dec 1816, by William Capers. Georgetown Meth Ch

Huber, Jacob & Anna Kuhn, 21 Aug 1803. St Matthews Luth Ch

Hudson, John of Charleston, mariner, & Ann Wish, of Charleston, spinster, to Rev. Richard Furman, 15 Jan 1811. Chaston ML

Hudson, Wm. & Rebekah Walden, 1 Oct 1818. Bryan Journal

Huger, Alfred, Esquire of Charleston, & Miss Sarah Rutledge, 10 April 1820. Holy Cross Ch

Huger, Benj. Dr. & Miss Jane Templar Bee, 15 May 1817 in Charleston. St Phil PR

Huger, Daniel Esqr. & Sarah Louisa Lance, daughter of Lambert Lance of Charleston, 28 Feb 1804; Parker Gough, trustee; Thomas Cooper, William Lance, wit. Mar Set 4: 380-385

Huger, Daniel E. & Isabella J. Middleton, daughter of Arthur Middleton, decd., 23 May 1801; Henry Middleton, trustee; Thos Morris, Henry M. Rutledge, wit. Mar Set 4: 62-65

Huger, Francis Capt., of Waccamaw, & Miss Harriot Lucas Pinckney, Santee, 14 Jan 1802. St Phil PR

Huggins, John & Clarissa Munding, license dated 27 May 1807; married 8 June 1807, by Enos James, M. of G. Darl MB

Hughes, Arthur of St. Bartholomews Parish, Colleton District, & Sophia Ferguson, of same, widow of James Edward Ferguson, 25 Aug 1806; Elizabeth Verlin, Susanna L. Hughes, trustees; Elizabeth Bearfield, Ann Ferguson, Margaret Wells, wit. Mar Set 5: 258-261

Hume, Alex Dr. & Miss Mary Morris, 29 April 1817 in Charleston. St Phil PR

Hume, Robert of Charleston, planter, & Ann-Eliza Moore, of Charleston, spinster, to Rev. Theodore Dehon, 21 May 1811. Chaston ML

Humphries, Richard of Charleston, mariner & Mary Buckle, __ March 1816; Lewis H. C. Schutt, trustee; John Black, Lewis Roux, wit. Mar Set 7: 40-42

Humphries, Richard W. & Miss Mary Buckle, 26 March 1816 in Charleston. St Phil PR

Hunnicutt, Willis, & Catherine McGuffin, 6 June 1820; William Carson, Esq., trustee; Mrs. Sarah McGuffin, mother of Catherine; Joseph Grisham, William Miller, wit. Pen DB P, p. 112

Hunt, Thomas, attorney & Mary Jennings, of Charleston, 21 Jan 1800; George Smith, Adam Tunno, trustees; Ann Mitchell, Wm. Clement, wit. Mar Set 3: 482-489

Hunter, John L. of Charleston, & Sarah E. Bowler, of Prince Williams Parish, 3 July 1816; Barkley Ferguson, William Frampton, Arthur Hughes, trustees; Barnardus M. Gilbert, William E. Ferguson, wit. Mar Set 7: 63-65

Hunter, John L. & wife, formerly Sarah E. Bowler, 1 Feb 1820; William Aiken, Esqr., of Charleston, merchant, trustee; Arthur Hughs, Wm. Hampton, L. E. Hughes, wit. Mar Set 8: 88-92

Hunter, Thomas, & Margaret Wright, license dated 17 Aug 1803; married by James Coleman, M. G. Darl MB

Hutchinson, Hugh, master of the ship Amity, & Miss Ann Peyton, of Charleston, 3 Oct 1800; Hugh Hutchenson, Geo. White, Hy. Peyton, wit. Mar Set 4: 32-33

Hutchinson, Mathias of Parish of St. George Dorchester,
   & Esther Roberts of same, spinster, 23 Dec 1802;
   Peter Robert, of St. Stephens Parish, planter, trustee;
   P. A. Smith, H. S. Poyas, wit. Mar Set 4: 258-264

Hutson, Isham & Catherine Smoke, 9 April 1818. Bryan
   Journal

Hutson, Richard W. of Prince Williams Parish, & Mary O'-
   Riely Ferguson, of Charleston, 2 June 1814; Elizabeth
   Milner Ferguson, Hon. Charles J. Colcock, trustees;
   M. Colcock, Sarah E. Anderson, wit. Mar Set 6: 327-
   331

Hutson, William, of Charleston, millwright, & Mary Ann
   Miller, of the same place, spinster, 8 Nov 1800. St
   Phil PR

Hyams, Henry of Charleston, & Judy Myers, of same, 18
   March 1813; Jacob Deleon, Chapman Moses, wit. Mar
   Set 6: 220-222

Hyams, Solomon of Charleston, vendue master, & Catharine
   Jacobs of same, widow and shop keeper, 17 June 1811;
   Capt. Myer Moses, trustee; E. N. Carvalko, minister
   of the Hebrew congregation, wit. Mar Set 6: 41-45

Hynes, John of St. Jas. Parish, Goosecreek, planter, &
   Martha Moore, of Pendleton Dist., spinster, 7 Feb
   1816; license to Rev. Dr. William Percy. Chaston Pro
   J

Ioor, Benjamin G. of Claremont County, Sumter District,
   & Sarah C. Walter, of Clarendon County, Sumter Dist-
   rict, 1 Nov 1810; Laurence Manning, Jno Potts, wit.
   Misc Rec B, pp. 702-703

Ioor, Benjamin G. & Miss Sarah Cantey Walter, of Clarendon, 1 Nov 1810, by Rev. John Jacob Tschudy. Holy
   Cross Ch

Ioor, John of Sumter District, & Emily Richardson of
   Georgetown, 21 March 1804; Peter Horry of Georgetown,
   and William Richardson & John Smyth Richardson of
   Sumter Dist., trustees; Samuel Fley, wit. Misc Rec
   B, pp. 289-295

Irby, John & Elizabeth Dewitt, to Rev. Joshua Lewis, 22
   June 1803. Marlboro ML

Irick, Volentine & Anna Mary Gates, 24 Nov 1800. St
   Matthews Luth Ch

Irvin, John S. D., planter, & Mary Crawford, widow, 12
Aug 1816; David Irvin, trustee; Charles Atkins Jr.,
Daniel Cole, Mary S. Irvin, wit. Mar Set 7: 71-73

Irving, Thomas & Sophia Shannon, 31 May 1810. Moses
Waddel

Izard, Ralph Stead & Esther Middleton, daughter of the
late Thomas Middleton, Esqr., 31 Oct 1811; Ralph
Izard Jr., Arthur Middleton, trustees; Thos. Mills,
H. M. Haig, wit. Mar Set 6: 90-91

Izard, Ralph-Stead of Charleston, planter, & Esther Middleton, of Charleston, spinster, to Rev. Thomas Mills,
30 Oct 1811. Chaston ML

Izard, Henry & Claudia Smith, 2 May 1814 in Charleston.
St Phil PR

Jackson, Edward & Rebecca Fitzpatrick, 19 July 1801. St
Matthews Luth Ch

Jack, servant of Mr. Datty, & Betsy, servant of Mr. Hall,
12 May 1816. St Mary's RC

Jackson, Henry Dr. & Martha J. Cobb, 16 Sept 1819. Moses
Waddel

Jackson, Josiah & Maryan Chalbo, spinster, 11 Nov 1800.
St Phil PR

Jackson, Montague of Charleston, & Hannah Hyams, spinster,
21 Feb 1811; Jervis Henry Stevens, Solomon Hyams,
trustees; John S. Cogdell, Eliazer Elizer, wit. Mar
Set 6: 27-28

Jackson, Thomas & Mary Anne Duncan, 13 Jan 1818. St
Mary's RC

Jackson, William, soldier, and Margaret Jurdon, widow,
19 July 1800. St Phil PR

Jackson, Zebulon and Mary Gutriage, 27 July 1801, John
Jackson, surety. York Pro 66/3125

James, slave of Mrs. George Matthews & Elizabeth, slave
of Mrs. George Matthews, 19 August 1813, in Charleston. St Phil PR

James & Clarissa, slave of Mr. Jno Smyth, 20 Dec 1815 in
Charleston. St Phil PR

James, Holloway, & Roxanna Howard, 15 March 1819; Stephen
D. Miller, wit. Proved in Richland Dist. Misc Rec D,
p. 107

Jay, Thomas, son of John Jay, Newberry Co., S. C., & Mary
Pearson, daughter of Thomas Pearson, 29 Jan 1800.
Bush R MM

Jean, Pierre & Marie Louise, servant of Mrs. LeBrieor,
16 May 1816. St Mary's RC

Jenings, John of Maryland, resident of Charleston, & Mary
Margaret Burges, of Charleston, widow of James Burges,
merchant, 9 Marcy 1808; Thomas Winstanley, attorney,
trustee; Em. Stephens, Jno Macnamara, wit. Mar Set
5: 389-392

Jenkins, Charles J. of St. Luke's Parish, & Mrs. Mary S.
Pelot, widow, 18 Jan 1816; Dr. Francis Y. Porcher of
St. Peters Parish, trustee; James Porcher, James
Postell Jr., wit. Mar Set 6: 423-425

Jenkins, Charles Jones of St. Lukes Parish, Beaufort
District, and wife Susan Emily, 11 June 1805; John
Kenny, trustee; Wm. M. Hutson, Geo. Taylor, wit. Mar
Set 5: 21-25

Jenkins, Elias of Charleston, brick-layer, & Mrs. Elizabeth Austin, of the same place, widow, 21 June 1800.
St Phil PR

Jenkins, John Col. of Parish of St. Helena, Beaufort
Dist., & Elizabeth Mary Ann Girardeau, widow, of St.
Bartholomew's Parish, Colleton Dist., 6 Sept 1817;
Peter B. Girardeau, trustee; John Jenkins, wit. Mar
Set 8: 27-31

Jim, slave of Mr. Yates, & Dye, slave of Mrs. M. Muraro,
11 Sept 1819 in Charleston. St Phil PR

Johans, Joseph & Marie Panpalon, 27 Dec 1815. St Mary's
RC

John, slave of Mr. Edmundston & Sarah, slave of Miss
Good, 26 Sept 1815 in Charleston. St Phil PR

John, slave of Benjamin Leese & Amarenthia, slave of
Samuel E. Axson, 4 June 1813, in Charleston. St Phil
PR

John & Phillis, slaves of Mr. P. T. Marchant, 6 Sept 1818
in Charleston. St Phil PR

John, slave of Mrs. Mathews & Moll, slave of Miss Fraser,
6 Jan 1819 in Charleston. St Phil PR

Johnson, Andre & Mrs. Lydia E. Hayes, 10 May 1818 in
Charleston. St Phil PR

Johnson, David of Charleston, gentleman, & Eleanor Clement, of the same place, spinster, 18 Dec 1800. St Phil PR

Johnson, James, of London, mariner, and Elizabeth Will, of Charleston, widow, 3 Feb 1801. St Phil PR

Johnson, James Slidell of Charleston, attorney, and Eleanor Sophia Reid, 5 April 1820; Robert Bentham, trustee; Thos. D. Condy, N. H. Boylston, wit. Mar Set 8: 101-110

Johnson, John & Miss Harriet Wilkins, 30 Oct 1815 in Charleston. St Phil PR

Johnson, John of Charleston, carpenter, & Ann Smith, widow of Archibald Smith Jr., decd., 1 Feb 1805; John M. Davis, William Wightman, Esqrs., trustees; John D. River, Joseph Moore, wit. Mar Set 4: 540-544

Johnson, Jonathan & Ann Mecklin, 5 June 1810. Moses Waddel

Johnson, Joshua & Rosa Berney, free persons of color, 7 Oct 1813, in Charleston. St Phil PR

Johnson, Peter & Ann Corkell, widow, 19 Oct 1815; Jeremiah Jessop, trustee; Thos Towle, Christopher Nelson, wit. Mar Set 6: 408-413

Johnson, Roswell Port of New Orleans, Louisiana, & Martha Seabrook Jenkins, of S. C.. spinster, granddaughter of Providence Bush of Edisto Island, 23 July 1817; John R. Mathews, wit. Mar Set 7: 200-202

Johnson, William & Sarah Tennehill, 30 March 1809. Moses Waddel

Johnson, Wm. & Sally Mills, 7 Aug 1803. Bryan Journal

Johnson, Wm & Miss Elizabeth Cox, 7 Feb 1816, in St. James Santee. St Phil PR

Johnston, Archibald Simpson, of Charleston & Agnes Bolton Ewing, daughter of Adam Ewing, late of Charleston, decd., 8 April 1807; James Ewing, John Ewing, Robert William Ewing, David Lamb Sr., wit. Mar Set 5: 291-295

Johnston, George of St. Stephens Parish, & Ann Bass of same, single woman, 24 June 1801; Gabriel Gignilliat & Daniel Kelly, trustee; John Herron, Robert Burdell, Thos Wait, wit. Mar Set 4: 79-81

Johnston, James, slave of Wm. H. Maguire, & Dolly, slave
of Mr. P. Smith, 11 Feb 1819 in Charleston. St Phil PR

Jones, Alexander & Mary Hyrne Smith, daughter of Thomas
Smith Senr., 3 Dec 1804; James S. Adams, Anchar Smith,
George Smith, Savage Smith, trustees; Isaac Minus,
wit. Mar Set 4: 475-477

Jones, Edward, physician, & Rachel Roberts, widow, daughter of James Jamison, decd., 1 July 1809; James Wood,
trustee. Mar Set 5: 523-526

Jones, Henry & Frances Gantt, 1 April 1804. Moses
Waddel

Jones, James & Mary Darby, 26 Dec 1816. Bryan Journal

Jones, Nathan & Sarah Powell, widow of Catfish, 15 Oct
1809(?). Marion ML

Jones, Peter & Abigil Duffey (col'd persons, free), 20
April 1815 in Charleston. St Phil PR

Jones, Richard Henry & Elizabeth Margaret Glover, 19 Dec
1815, in Charleston. St Phil PR

Jones, Stephen & Jane Caldwell, 15 Nov 1810. Moses
Waddel

Jones, Thomas of Charleston, factor & Eliza Troup of
same, widow, 12 Jan 1810; Robert Dorrill, William
Dewees Junr, trustees; Thos S. Nowell, Eliza Pagett,
wit. Mar Set 5: 513-515

Jones, Thomas & Martha P. Mosely, 13 Feb 1813. Moses
Waddel

Jones, Thomas & Eliza Darracott, 13 April 1815. Moses
Waddel

Jones, Thomas of Charleston, factor, & Eliza Troup, of
Charleston, widow, to Rev. James D. Simons, 13 Jan
1810. Chaston ML

Jones, William & Mary Thorne, 15 March 1801. Moses
Waddel

Jones, William & Mary M. Talbot, 10 April 1816. Moses
Waddel

Jordan, Martin & Maria Gallagher, 23 April 1816. St.
Mary's RC

Joseph & Catharine, slaves of Dr. Poyas, 30 Nov 1811, in
St. Philip's Parish. St Phil PR

Joseph, servant of Mr. Robey, & Dorothee, servant of Mr. Courtier, 8 May 1816. St Mary's RC

Joseph, Isaac, son of Lazarus & Betsy Joseph, and Rebecca Wellcome, daughter of Benjamin and Sarah Wellcome, 6 April 1808, Island of St. Thomas; Gomez Cadet, wit. married by Abraham M. Monsanto, 6 April 1808. Mar Set 7: 162-164

Josephs, Levy L. of Georgetown, & Miss Frances Joseph, daughter of Lizar Joseph of same, 5 Jan 1820; Israel Solomons, Joseph Josephs, trustees; Walter H. Perry, Nathan Emanuel, wit. Mar Set 8: 83

Jowitt, John & Miss Eliza Guy, 6 Sept 1818 in Charleston. St. Phil PR

Keating, William of Charleston & Elizabeth Crowley, of same, 24 April 1802; Edward Lynah, trustee; Henry Bailey, Geo. Robt. Logan, wit. Mar Set 4: 185-189

Kelly, Christopher & Elizabeth M'Divett, 21 Aug 1817 in Charleston. St Phil PR

Kelly, Marcus N. of Charleston, & Rebecca O'Hara, 24 Feb 1820; Charles O'Hara, Henry O'Hara, trustees; Jane Patteson, Joseph Coppinger, wit. Mar Set 8: 144-147

Kelly, Marcus N. & Miss Rebecca O'Hara, 24 Feb 1820 in Charleston. St Phil PR

Kelly, Moses, Newberry Dist., S. C., & Mary Teague, 17 Sept 1800. Bush R MM

Kelly, Thomas & Ann Corbin, 3 Jan 1811. Bryan Journal

Kendall, & Lucy, slaves of Mrs. Smith, 7 Jan 1814, in Charleston. St Phil PR

Kennan, Henry & Rebecca Mege (formerly Rebecca Morris), 16 June 1804; Peter Freneau, Moses Winstanley, trustees; Jas. Delaire, Thos W. Legge, wit. Mar Set 4: 441-445

Kennedy, Benjamin & Lucy Gibert, 29 July 1818. Moses Waddel

Kennedy, Edward of Charleston, & Elizabeth Hutchinson of Chehaw, spinster, 11 May 1803; Spencer Man, Fratz Jacob Foltz, trustees; Thos D. Bladen, wit. Mar Set 4: 369-372

Kennedy, John & Jane McCollough, 22 Aug 1805. Bryan Journal

Kennedy, Lionel Henry of Charleston, attorney at law, to
Mary-Ann Jane Stevens, of Charleston, spinster, to
Rev. James D. Simons, 8 June 1811. Chaston ML

Kennerly, Thomas & Rebecca Whetstone, 29 Dec 1801. St
Matthews Luth Ch

Kenworthy, John, son of Joshua & Mary Kenworthy, & Rebekah Cook, daughter of Isaac & Sarah Cook, decd., 26
Nov 1801. Cane Cr MM

Kershaw, James & Lydia Ann Vaughan, 8 May 1813. Kershaw
Diary

Kershaw, John & Harriet Dubose, 22 Oct 1812. Kershaw
Diary

Kilburn, Dr. Samuel & Mrs. Mary Burch, widow, of Great
Pee Dee, 7 Oct 1811. Marion ML

Kilrey, John & Mary Ann Carroll, __ July 1819. St Mary's
RC

Kimball, George, of Charleston, & Eliza Gordon, daughter
of James Gordon, merchant, decd., 29 July 1808; George
Kimball, Martha Gordon, widow of James Gordon, trustees;
Phoebe Kelser, Sarah Rouldin, wit. Mar Set 5: 402-406

Kimball, George, of Charleston, merchant, & Eliza Gordon,
of Charleston, spinster, 29 July 1808, to Rev. Richard Furman. Chaston ML

King, Leonard of Charleston, house carpenter, & Elizabeth
Bride, widow, 9 Sept 1815; Josias James Dupre, trustee; William Payne, wit. Mar Set 7: 77-83

Kinloch, Frederick of Charleston, son of Francis Kinloch
and Mary I'on Lowndes, eldest daughter of Thomas
Lowndes, 21 March 1816; Keat. Lewis Simons, Jacob
Bond I'on, wit. Mar Set 7: 59-63

Kinloch, Frederick & Miss Mary I'on Lowndes, 21 March
1816 in Charleston. St Phil PR

Kinloch, George & Miss Charlotte Granby, 8 Dec 1816 in
Charleston. St Phil PR

Kinloch, Richmond of Charleston, millwright, & Sophia
Jeanerette Hopton, of Charleston, spinster, 3 March
1819; license to Revd. Frederick Dalcho. Chaston Pro J

Kirk, Isaac, Newberry Dist., S. C., & Rebekah Jinkins,
widow of Isaac Jinkins, 4 Nov 1802. Bush R MM

SOUTH CAROLINA MARRIAGES 1800-1820

Kirkwood, George & Jane Calhoun, 21 April 1814. Moses
Waddel

Kleckley, Jacob & Christenah Coogle, 13 April 1813. St.
Michaels Luth Ch

Knight, Thomas, son of Solomon & Elizabeth Knight, decd.,
Richmond Co., N. C. & Christian Thomas, daughter of
John & Molley Thomas, Marlborough Co., S. C., 26 Jan
1804. Piney Grove MM

Knox, John & Miss Elizabeth Pritchard, 2 Aug 1810, in St.
Philip's Parish. St Phil PR

Knox, John of Georgetown, & Charlotte P. Simons, of Williamsburgh District, 5 May 1808; Francis Green of Georgetown Dist., trustee; Francis M. Baxter, Saml R. Mouzon,
wit. Mar Set 5: 399-402

Koger, Joseph the younger, of St. Bartholomew's Parish,
& Abigail Milhouse, widow of John Milhous the younger,
decd., 25 March 1802; Francis McHugh, Anthy. Newton,
wit. Mar Set 4: 180-185

Kohne, Frederick of Charleston, merchant, & Eliza Neuf-
ville of same, spinster, _____ 1807; John Elias
Moore, Adam Gilchrist, Esqrs., trustees; Edwd Mitchell,
Wm Hasell Gibbes, wit. Mar Set 5: 316-333

Koon, Samuel & Mary Ann Dupryee, 9 Dec 1819. Drehr
Journal

Kunhardt, William of Charleston, merchant, & Deborah
Halliday, of Charleston, spinster, to Rev. James D.
Simons, 20 Sept 1810. Chaston ML

LaBruce, Joseph & Catherine J. Ward, daughter of Joshua
Ward, 6 May 1819; Joshua Ward Jr., Benjn Huger, all of
Dist. of Georgetown, trustees; Robt Withers, John F.
Pyatt, John Ward Mathews, wit. Mar Set 8: 34-37

Lacoste, Charles, of Charleston, merchant, & Clotilde-
Gabriele-Emelie de Rochefort, of Charleston, spinster,
to Rev. S. F. Gallagher, 4 Sept 1809. Chaston ML

Ladeveze, Joseph Victor & Marie Ann Tenet, 9 Oct 1813.
St Mary's RC

Ladson, James of St. Bartholomews Parish, & Florence Waring Smith, daughter of Archar Smith, of the Parish of
Goose Creek, 6 May 1800; William Boone Mitchell, James
Boone, of St. Pauls Parish, trustees; Morton Waring,
wit. Mar Set 3: 462-464

Ladson, James of St. Bartholomews Parish, Colleton Dist., & Elizabeth Day, daughter of William Day, Esqr., of same, 1 Sept 1802; O'Brien Smith, William Boone Mitchell, Richard Singellton the younger, trustees; Ann Postell, wit. Mar Set 4: 233-235

LaFay, Jean & Marie Louise LaFon, __ July 1811. St Mary's RC

Lafond, Francis C. N. of Charleston, goldsmith, & Sophia Smith, of Charleston, widow, 7 Dec 1813; license to Christopher Gadsden. Chaston Pro J

Laford, Francis C. N. & Sophia Smith, col'd persons, 9 Dec 1813, in Charleston. St Phil PR

Laight, Edward W. of City of New York, & Miss Ann Elliott Huger of Charleston, 22 Apr 1802; William Lowndes, Daniel E. Huger, wit. Mar Set 4: 264-268

Laight, Edward William, Esq. of New York, and Ann Elliott Huger, of Charleston, spinster, 22 April 1802. St Phil PR

Lamar, Charles & Mary Clitheral (people of color), 9 April 1812, in Charleston, by the Revd. Mr. Fowler. St Phil PR

Lambright, James & Martha S. Collins, Barnwell Dist., 3 June 1814; Stephen Smith, George W. Collins, trustees; James Wilson, J. Robison Junr., Wilson Brown, wit. Misc Rec C, pp. 139-141

Lamy, Louis Vincent & Marianne May, 22 April 1809. St Mary's RC

Lance, Francis B. & Elizabeth Jane Styles Ball, 30 Nov 1819; Mrs. Elizabeth St. John Ball, widow, trustee; William Lance, John Gough Lance, wit. Mar Set 8: 60-62

Lance, Francis & Elizabeth Ball, 18 Nov 1819 in Charleston. Pr Geo Winyaw

Lance, Maurice H. of Georgetown, minister of the gospel, & Anna Maria Allston, 13 Nov 1816; Benjamin Allston, William W. Trapier, John M. Taylor, trustees; Mary C. Allston, Jno Keith, wit. Mar Set 7: 123-126

Landrum, Isham & Jemima Tennehill, 14 April 1815. Moses Waddell

Lang, Thos. & Mary McRa, 29 March 1815. Kershaw Diary

Lang, Wm. W. & Kitty Boykin, 19 Feb 1814. Kershaw Diary

Langton, John of Charleston, gentleman, & Susannah Elizabeth Hildrup of Charleston, widow, 31 Dec 1812; Joshua Brown, merchant, trustee. Mar Set 6: 186-191

Langton, John & Mrs. Susannah Hilldrup, 16 Feb 1813, in Charleston. St Phil PR

Lansdell, Benjamin Cooper, & Carolina Geffkon, 13 Oct 1814. 2d Pres Ch

Lapenne, John A. & Louise Ursula Lacroix, 20 Feb 1819. St Mary's RC

Lapenne, Joseph, merchant, son of Jn. Bte. Lapenne, and wife Elizabeth Geoffroy, & Marie Eve Hofman, widow, of Valentine Erwin (?), (no date, recorded 2 July 1812), (original in French). Mar Set 6: 145-148

Lapenne, Joseph & Elizabeth Riboulot, 24 June 1816. St Mary's RC

Laraste, Charles & Emilie Rockefort, 4 Sept 1809. St Mary's RC

Laroque, Bernard & Marie Louise Arquier, 28 Jan 1816. St Mary's RC

Laval, Jacint Jr., of Charleston & Frances Susannah Rivers, daughter of William Rivers Senr., planter, decd., 1 Nov 1804; William Yeadon, Esqr., attorney, trustee; Eliza Ainger, Ann Rivers, wit. Mar Set 4: 512-519

Laval, Lewis & Maria _____, 8 May 1817, by William Capers. Georgetown Meth Ch

Laval, Louis of Charleston Dist., & Mary A. Belin of Georgetown, 7 May 1817; Jno Withers Junr., A. D. Murray, wit. Mar Set 7: 215-216

Lawrence, Samuel & Harriet Guerard of Beaufort Dist., 12 March 1814; Robert L. D. Treville, trustee; Saml Reid, Milton Maxcy, wit. Mar Set 6: 318-320

Lawrence, Samuel & Elizabeth Colman, of St. Helenas Parish, town of Beaufort, widow, 1 June 1820; George W. Morrall, trustee; Peter Alrich, Morris Barnard, wit. Mar Set 8: 153-156

Lawrence, Samuel & Elizabeth Givens, widow, 18 Jan 1800. St Hel PR

Lawrence, Sam'l Senr & Elizabeth Capers Ellis, 18 Jan 1801. St Hel PR

Lawson, Capt. John, mariner & Mary A. Danford, spinster,
1 June 1803; Edmond Green, Saltus Lawson, trustees;
Mary Keen, Eliza Danford, Andrew Hasell, wit. Mar Set
4: 309-312

Leavensworth, Melines C. of Edgefield Dist., planter, &
Ann LaMar of same, widow of Thomas LaMar, or Horse
Creek, 4 June 1803; Luke Smith & Thomas Lamar Jr.,
trustees; Sarah Lamar & Chas Goodwin, wit. Misc Rec
B, pp. 222-228

Lebby, Robert of Charleston, gent., & Catharine Ecklin
Lees, widow, 5 Sept 1800; Ralph Grattan, gent., trustee; Ann Eliza Grattan, Richard Howard, wit. Mar Set
3: 489-492

Lebby, William, of Charleston, ship-wright, & Frances-
Sarah Scott, of Charleston, spinster, 13 May 1809.
Chaston ML

Lecompte, Jean Pierre Phillip & Marie Bodine Modeste
Bizeul, 9 July 1815. St Mary's RC

LeCourtois, Anthony Thomas & Elizabeth Kuntz, 1 July 1809.
St Mary's RC

Lee, Mr. & Eady Jourdain, 24 Dec 1801. Kershaw Diary

Lee, Andrew & Peggy N. Harper, 7 Jan 1808. Moses Waddel

Lee, Francis of Charleston & Ann Lee Beckman, daughter of
Samuel Beckman, decd., 30 April 1812; William Lee,
Robert Howard, Stephen Lee, Paul H. S. Lee, trustees;
Tho. Lee, Jno M. Lee, wit. Mar Set 6: 134-139

Lee, James and Eliza Jones, free persons of color, 10
May 1819 in Charleston. St Phil PR

Lee, Stephen & Elizabeth Gibert, 8 March 1815. Moses
Waddel

Lege, Jean Marie & Marie Francoise St. Romes, 16 June
1814. St Mary's RC

Leggett, Henry C. of Marion Dist., & Miss Anna Hazelden
of the same neighbourhood, 6 Sept 1809; married by
Philip Kirton, 7 Sept 1809. Marion ML

Leggette, Henry C. & Mrs. Anny Heazelden, 4 Sept 1809;
William Heazelden Senr., sec. Marion ML

Leith, William & ____ Atwood, 23 Dec 1800. Moses Waddel

Leland, Aaron Withney, of Christ-Church Parish, Reverend, & Eliza Hibben, of Christ-Church Parish, spinster, to Rev. Isaac S. Keith, 10 May 1809. Chaston ML

Lemacke, John J., Esqr., of St. Bartholomew's Parish, Colleton Dist., & Harriet M. Walter of same, daughter of Jacob Walter decd., 24 Jan 1816; William Walter, trustee; Jas. M. Ford, Frederick C. Witsell, James Bowman, wit. Mar Set 7: 47-48

Lemon, James & Louisa Crofts, 13 Jan 1814. 2d Pres Ch

Leon, Louis Francois & Elisabeth Dorothe DeVille, 2 April 1816. St Mary's RC

Leroi, Francis & Rose Brown, colored persons, 5 Jan 1820. St Mary's RC

LeRoy, Peter & Anne Beattie, 1 July 1819. Moses Waddel

LeRoy, Zavile & Julia, widow of Louis Mege, of Charleston, 2 March 1806; Moses Davega; Isaac DaCosta, wit. Mar Set 5: 148-149

Lespinas, Jean Baptiste, merchant, native of Rochelle, dept. de la Charente, son of Francois Lespinas & wife Ann Chaten, both deceased, & Felicite Anmaistre, refugee from St. Domingo, native of Limbe, Isle et Cote, S. Domingo, daughter of Jacques Anmaistre & wife Madelaine Glaumont, deceased, 22 Oct 1819. (original in French). Mar Set 6: 113-116

Lespinas, Jean Baptiste & Felicite Aumaistre, 18 Oct 1810. St Mary's RC

Leverett, W. A. & Catharina Henrietta Eudalia Grenguet, 10 Dec 1809. St Mary's RC

Levy, Eliazer & Miss Anna Abraham, 27 Dec 1801; Moses Danega, Saml Hyams, wit. Mar Set 4: 104

Levy, George & Hannah Jackson, widow, of Charleston, 12 June 1817; Henry Hyams, trustee, Moses Davis, Solomon Hyams, wit. Mar Set 7: 189-192

Lewellin, Richard M. & Lettice Winn, _____ 1802. Moses Waddel

Lewis, slave of the Miss Huger, & Silvia, slave of Mrs. Gregorie, 22 Dec 1812. St Phil PR

Lewis, Caleb, son of Thomas decd & Martha Lewis, of Colleton Dist., S. C., & Susannah Cook, daughter of Isaac & Charity Cook, 29 April 1802. Bush R MM

Lewis, John & Cecile Henriette Durioux, 16 Feb 1812. St
   Mary's RC

Lewis, John & Sarah Williamson (free), 25 Dec 1817, at
   Georgetown. Pro Geo Winyaw

Lewis, John & Mrs. Sarah A. Annely, 9 May 1819 in Charleston. St Phil PR

Lide, Robert and Frances Wright, to Rev. Joshua Lewis,
   _____ 1800. Marlboro ML

Liepman, Ezekiel of St. John's Parish, merchant, & Sarah
   Thomas Benoist, spinster, daughter of Philip Benoist,
   17 Feb 1817; Solomon Legare, William Yeadon, trustees;
   Mary Carr, John Gates, wit. Mar Set 7: 128-134

Lilly, Cyrus, free man & Joane, slave of Mrs. Ferguson,
   22 sept 1818 in Charleston. St Phil PR

Lilly, Rev. Samuel of Georgetown & Margarett Mitchell of
   St. John's Parish, widow, 30 April 1807; Francis Marshall of Georgetown, M. D., William Nesbitt Mitchell
   of St. John's Parish, trustees; William North, Robt
   Collins, wit. Mar Set 5: 302-305

Lindsay, William of Charleston, merchant, & Sarah Teasdale, of St Andrew, spinster, to Rev. Edmond Matthews,
   29 Dec 1810. Chaston ML

Ling, John of Charleston, merchant, & Mary-Ann Jones of
   Charleston, spinster, to Rev. William Percy, 4 May
   1809. Chaston ML

Lockart, John of Charleston & Eliza Waltz, 7 July 1819;
   Peter Artman, trustee; Thomas Jno Gantt, wit. Mar
   Set 8: 44-46

Lockwood, Thomas Perkins and wife Mary Sophia (formerly
   Mary Sophia Postell, daughter of Col. Benjamin Postell,
   late of St. Bartholomew's Parish, decd), 20 Aug 1817;
   Richard Henry Fishburne, Paul S. H. Lee, trustees;
   Elizabeth Fishburne, George Evans, John Sanders, wit.
   Mar Set 7: 205-208

London, Francis & Miss Mary Clarke, 1 Nov 1813, by Rev.
   George Strebeck. Holy Cross Ch

Long, Felix & Maria Bennett, 23 Dec 1817. 2d Pres Ch

Long, Richard H. & Ann G. Hay, 10 Nov 1813. Moses Waddel

Longworth, Archibald of St. Luke's Parish, & Mary Magdalene Dupont of same, 19 Dec 1812; Joseph Longworth, trustee; Frances Dupont, Fortunatus Bryan, wit. Mar Set 6: 181-184

Longworth, Joseph of State of Georgia, and Elizabeth Leacraft, of St. Luke's Parish, widow, 28 Nov 1808; Charles Black of S. C., trustee; Mary Bowman, Jabez Longworth, George McNony, wit. Mar Set 5: 454-456

Loper, Isaac & Eliza. Nusom, widow, 22 Dec 1808. Bryan Journal

Lopez, William & Catherine Lee (free persons of color), 6 June 1815, in Charleston. St Phil PR

Lord, Archibald Brown of Charleston & Mary Waties, of same, 22 Nov 1810; Erasmus Rothmahler, Jacob Belser, trustees; J. Wilson, W. J. Gunning, wit. Mar Set 6: 1-2

Lord, Archibald-Brown, of Charleston, Esquire, & Mary G. Waites, of Charleston, spinster, to Rev. James D. Simons, 10 Nov 1810. Chaston ML

Lovell, Josiah Sturges & Hannah Francis Poinsett of Charleston, spinster, 24 May 1806; John Roberts Poinsett, John Johnston, trustees; Jno M. Davis, Josiah Sturges, wit. Mar Set 5: 212-217

Lowndes, William, Esq., of Charleston, gentleman, & Miss Elizabeth Pinckney, of the same place, spinster, 10 Sept 1802. St Phil PR

Lowrey, Isham & Mary Ann Rebekah Brown, of St. Bartholomew's Parish, 4 Nov 1817; Saml Lewis, John L. Chaplin, James W. Monk, wit. Mar Set 7: 274-275

Lowther, Saml & Ann S. Pepper, of St. Luke's Parish, Beaufort Dist., 16 Jan 1814; Susan G. Bourquin, trustee; Geo J. Logan, Daniel P. Pepper, wit. Mar Set 6: 325-327

Lucas, William of Charleston, Esquire, & Charlotte Hume, of Charleston, spinster, 29 Sept 1819; license to Revs. Mr. Robert S. Symes. Chaston Pro J

Luther, Simeon of Charleston, shoe-maker, & Mary Mood of Charleston, spinster, 24 Dec 1811. Chaston ML

Lynah, Edward & Miss Eliza Fickling, 27 Nov 1816 in Charleston. St Phil PR

Lynah, James & Miss Emma Parker, 15 Oct 1816 in Charleston. St Phil PR

McBride, David S. & Sophia Rumney, 15 April 1817; George
W. Towers, trustee; F. Dupont, Joseph P. Rumney, wit.
married 5 April 1817 by Jno Crawford, E. M. E. C.,
St. Luke's Parish. Mar Set 7: 197-199

M'Bride, James L. Dr. & Miss Ellinor Gourdin, 4 March 1811,
at Pineville in St. Stephen's Parish. St Phil PR

Macbride, Robert, a free man of color, & Diana, slave of
Mrs. Joe Legare, 25 Dec 1820 in Charleston. St Phil PR

McBurney, Dr. Hugh of Jacksonborough, Colleton Dist., &
Elizabeth Thompson of the Round O, Colleton Dist., 18
Nov 1802; Thomas Fendin, Joseph Fuller, Phillip S.
Smith, trustees; W. Youngblood, Andrew H. Johnes, wit.
Mar Set 4: 270-274

McCall, Beekman, & Anna B. Ferguson, 20 Oct 1813, in St.
Philip's Church. St Phil PR

McCall, John of Charleston, grocer, & Mary Vesez, widow
of Charles Vesez, 24 Dec 1812; Samuel Jasper Wagner,
trustee; James Watts, Saml Canty, wit. Mar Set 6:
228-230

M'Cants, _____ & Mrs. Walker, 23 March 1813, in Charleston. St Phil PR

Macauley, George Junr. & Eliza Provaux, 24 Dec 1812 in
Charleston. St Phil PR

McCleish, James & Ann Williams, both of Charleston, 27
March 1813; Benjamin Porter, trustee; John Shelden,
John Saml Courtney, wit. Mar Set 6: 261-263

McColgan, Thomas & Priscilla St. Gray, 28 Oct 1819. St
Mary's RC

McCormick, Richard, of Charleston, gentleman, & Eliza
Holliday, of Charleston, spinster, to Rev. James D.
Simons, 20 Sept 1810. Chaston ML

McCulloch, William & Margery Lee, 9 May 1811. Moses
Waddel

McDonald, William of Williamsburgh Dist., & Emily Louisa
Couturier of St. John's Parish, Charleston Dist., widow, 27 Dec 1817; Elias Couturier, Robert J. Kirk,
trustees; Susan A. Gilliland, Frances Marion R. Mc-
Kelvey, wit. Mar Set 7: 230-233

M'Donald, William & Mrs. Emily Louise Couturier, 1 Jan
1818 in Charleston. St Phil PR

McDonnald, John & Mary Ann Noy, 28 Dec 1820. St Mary's RC

McDonnel, William Senr., commonly called County William,
& Nancy Smith, single woman, Abbeville District, 3
Oct 1814; Thomas Wiley, James Wiley, Alexander Wiley,
wit. Mar Set 6: 368-369

McDowell, John of Charleston, merchant, & Mary Braund, of
Charleston, widow, to Rev. William Percy, 18 Oct 1809.
Chaston ML

McElhenny, James, minister of the Gospel, John's Island,
& Susannah Wilkinson Jr., widow, 12 March 1800; Ed-
ward Wilkinson & Paul Hamilton, Esqrs., trustees; Jean
Slann, Margaret Jenkins, wit. Mar Set 3, pp. 434-435

McElvey, John & Betsy McElhenny, 22 July 1813. Moses
Waddel

McEwen, Patrick of Charleston, merchant, & Sarah Lothrop,
of Charleston, spinster, to Rev. James D. Simons, 16
Dec 1809. Chaston ML

McGehee, Carr & Charlotte Mosely, 23 July 1816. Moses
Waddel

McGehee, Meredith & Eliza Wilson, 2 June 1808. Moses
Waddel

McGehee, Meredith & Peggy Harper, 28 Oct 1813. Moses
Waddel

McGillivray, Alexander Hinckley of Charleston, & Eliza
Bampfield Geyer, 13 Feb 1813; John Hinckley Mitchell,
trustee. Mar Set 7: 182-183

McGilvery, Alexander, of Robeson Co., N. C., & Mary
Manderville of Marlboro, married by Rev. Daniel Smith,
7 Dec 1818. Marlboro ML

McGinley, Samuel of Philadelphia, Pa., & Jerusha McCann,
widow of Charleston, 23 Feb 1814; Peter Smith, of
Charleston, woodfactor, trustee; Chs. Fraser, Augt.
Winthrop, wit. Mar Set 6: 299-303

McGinn, Arthur & Maria England, 29 Nov 1817. St Mary's RC

McGrath, Robert & Nancy Wingfield, _____1800. Moses
Waddel

McGrill, John & Charlotte Gates, 16 Aug 1810. St Matthews Luth Ch

McIlhenny, Vincent & Mary Barksdale, 4 Dec 1817. Moses
Waddel

McKaskill, Peter, of Anson Co., N. C., & Nancy Rankin of
Marlboro, to Rev. David McKay, 13 Feb 1817. Marlboro
ML

Mackay, Franklin Paine & Martha Wood, 18 Jan 1820; Isaac
C. Moses, trustee; Hannah Moses, J. Moise, wit. Mar
Set 8: 78-82

McKay, George of St. Andrew's Parish, & Susanna Cheves,
12 July 1803; John Lee, Langdon Cheves, wit. Mar Set
4: 304-309

Mackay, Mungo of Edisto Island & Elizabeth Baynard, relict
of William Baynard decd., 23 Oct 1804; John Mikell
Senr., William Wood, trustees; John Patterson, Timothy
Kelly, wit. Mar Set 4: 478-481

McKiernan, James of Charleston, & Ann Desbeaux of same,
spinster, 31 Dec 1804; Adolphus Beckman, trustee;
John Gros, wit. Mar Set 4: 474-475

McKinley, Robert & Nancy Mathis, 16 Jan 1809. Moses
Waddel

McKinly, James & Eliza McCurdy, 13 Feb 1806. Moses
Waddel

McKinney, John & Nancy Horn, 13 March 1802, Matthew
McRight, surety. York Pro 66/3132

McLaughlan, Duncan, & Margaret Muldrou, 24 Sept 1804.
Darl MB

McLean, John & Miss Treascy Newsom of Little Pee Dee, 1
June 1813. Marion ML

McLeod, Hector Chisolm & Miss Frances Don Moubray, 28
Nov 1816 in Charleston. St Phil PR

McLinton, Robert & Nancy Breazeal, 10 Dec 1807. Moses
Waddel

McMullin, William & Susan Scott, 5 Oct 1813. Moses
Waddel

McNally, John & Elizabeth Harvey, 19 Aug 1819. St Mary's
RC

McNellage, Alex & Margaret Davis, 8 June 1815. Bryan
Journal

McNish, Henry of St. Luke's Parish, planter, & Jane D.
Dupont (married many years), & Have five daughters
living (named), 26 April 1816; Thomas E. Screven,
Thomas Baker, wit. Mar Set 7: 164-170

McOwen, Patrick of Charleston, merchant, & Sarah Lothrop, daughter of Seth Lothrop, Esqr., merchant, 19 Dec 1809; Samuel H. Lothrop, Robert Primrose, trustees; Jno Smith, James O Hear Junr., wit. Mar Set 5: 516-520

McRa, Powell & Mary Singleton, 10 Jan 1813. Kershaw Diary

McRae, Capt. John & Mary Johnston, spinster, 27 Feb 1806; license directed to Rev. John Wood. Marion ML

McTeer, John & Eliza Ulmer, 18 Jan 1816. Bryan Journal

Maguire, Thomas & Hester Solomons, colored persons, 13 May 1817 in Charleston. St Phil PR

Magwood, Charles A. & Miss Rebecca O'Hara, 16 March 1820 in Charleston. St Phil PR

Mahor, Louis & Luci Marie Anne Daudier, 27 Sept 1810. St Mary's RC

Maine, William & Miss Lydia Ann Gettner, 29 Sept 1817 in Charleston. St Phil PR

Mair, Patrick, of Charleston, merchant, & Martha Bigelow, spinster, 17 Nov 1801; Henry Bailey, attorney, trustee; C. Edmonston, John Ross, wit. Mar Set 4: 113-115

Man, Spencer John of Charleston, merchant & Ann Barksdale, relict of Thomas Jones Barksdale, late of Christ Church Parish, planter, & daughter of Thomas Ashby Esqr., of St. Thomas Parish, 10 July 1807; Thomas Ashby, William Shackelford, planters, trustees; Isaac Edwards, wit. Mar Set 5: 333-336

Manigault, Gabriel Henry & Miss Ann Heyward, 10 April 1817 in Charleston. St Phil PR

Marcel, Jacques Albert, bourgeois of Lauzanne, Switzerland, son of Paul Samuel Marcel and wife Suzanna Albertine Jacquelina Payen, and Claudine Armande Debat, minor daughter of Jean Martin Debat (recorded 1 May 1809). (Original in French). Mar Set 5: 445-451

Manson, Andrew of Brunswick, Ga., merchant, & Mary Hutchins, of Charleston, spinster, _____, 18__ (recorded 3 Dec 1812); Isaac A. Johnson, physician & Samuel S. Hutchins, bricklayer, trustees; Jos. Johnson, Alexr. W. Garden, wit. Mar Set 6: 162-166

March, Slave of E. B. Lining & Sally, slave of Ann M'-Lacklin, 2 Nov 1812, in Charleston. St Phil PR

March, Charles & Mary Hutchinson, widow of Thomas Hutchinson, 29 Dec 1818; Honora Pyne, trustee; James Bankhead, Anne Bankhead, wit. Mar Set 7: 334-337

Marchant, Peter T. & Miss Amelia I. Mitchell, people of color, 4 March 1818 in Charleston. St Phil PR

Marcus & Rose (free people), April 1817, at Georgetown. Pr Geo Winyaw

Margart, John Henry of Charleston, blacksmith, & Margaret Neithamar, of same, spinster, 25 June 1812; Charles Christian Philips, butcher, trustee; John Strohecker, John N. Martin, wit. Mar Set 6: 285-290

Marine, Charles, son of Jonathan & Mary Marine, Marlborough Co., S. C., & Abba Cox, daughter of Josiah & Judeth Cox, Richmond Co., N. C., 26 April 1804. Piney Grove MM

Marine, Jesse, son of Jonathan & Mary Marine, Marlborough Dist., S. C., & Phebe Cox, daughter of Josiah & Judah Cox, Richmond Co., N. C., 24 May 1804. Piney Grove MM

Marion, Nathaniel Wickum, of St. James Parish, Goosecreek, physician & Jane McCullers, 25 July 1818; Robert Matthews, trustee; Archer McKee, Richard Ashman, wit. Mar Set 7: 290-293

Marion, Nathaniel of St. John's Parish, & Mrs. Jane McCants, widow of Robert McCants, of same, planter, 26 Nov 1818; James Packer, Charles Cooper, wit. Mar Set 8: 12-14

Marshall, Francis of Georgetown, & Ann Wilson of same, 17 Nov 1803; Daniel O Hara, Thomas Chapman & William Grants, Esqrs., trustees; Wm. T. Knox, Saml. R. Mouzon, William North, wit. Mar Set 4: 455-461

Martin, Edmund & Elizabeth Ferguson, Beaufort Dist., 20 April 1815; Zacheus Ayer, Chas. Gillison, wit. Mar Set 6: 386

Martin, James & Rachel Parker, 18 Nov 1802. Bryan Journal

Martin, James & Eliza Harris, 19 July 1810. Moses Waddel

Martin, John & Sally Gowens, free persons of color, 3 Oct 1819 in Charleston. St Phil PR

Martin, John Gen. & Mary A. Barksdale, _____ May 1802. Moses Waddel

Martin, Johnson & Margaret Green, 4 March 1813. Moses Waddel

Martin, Leonard & Cathe. Lazenby, ___ March 1801. Moses
   Waddel

Martin, Pierre Louis (free) & Maire (slave), 10 Jan 1820.
   St Mary's RC

Mathews, Benjamin & Maria Croft, 11 April 1814; John Ward
   Mathews, William Mathews Jr., wit. Mar Set 6: 337-338

Mathews, John Raven of Charleston & Elizabeth Whalley,
   relict of ____ Whalley, decd., 28 March 1806; George
   Mathews, father of John Raven Mathews, and Christopher Jenkins, brother of sd. Elizabeth Whalley, trustees; Ann Fayssoux, Thomas Mathews, wit. Mar Set 5:
   207-211

Mathews, Joseph C. & Margaret Brock, 17 Sept 1807. Moses
   Waddel

Mathews, Rev. Philip of Charleston, and wife Frances, 20
   May 1805; Robert Smith Hort, William Joseph Bonhost,
   of Georgetown, trustees; Israel Munds, Francis G.
   Deliesseline, wit. Mar Set 5: 54-56

Mathews, Thomas & Harrie Edwards, both of Charleston, 3
   Oct 1805; Mrs. Rebecca Edwards, trustee; John Bee
   Holmes, wit. Mar Set 5: 191-193

Mathis, William of Camden, merchant, & Marriah Bracy, 7
   March 1820; James McGauchey, John G. McKinzie, trustees; John Duncan, Hugh McNeel, wit. Misc Rec D, pp.
   187-188

Matiss, Jean Pierre C. & Christine Morgenstein, 6 Sept
   1819. St Mary's RC

Matthews, Robert, of St. John, planter, & Alice-Kirk
   Hutchinson, of St. John, spinster, to Rev. Christr. E.
   Gadsden, 11 May 1809. Chaston ML

Matthiesen, Conrad Frederick & Josephine Felicity Sandos
   of Charleston, 6 June 1808; Jean Baptiste Le Breton,
   Jean Fredrick Sandos, trustees; Isaac Griggs, wit.
   Mar Set 5: 396-399

Matthieu, Andre & Mrs. Mary Reid, 5 Jan 1817 in Charleston. St Phil PR

Maurele, Mayol & Marie Victoire Venne Barbier, 10 March
   1812. St Mary's RC

Maury, Evariste & Anne Lambert, 17 April 1808. St Mary's
   RC

Maxcy, Milton & Mrs. Mary Barnwell, widow of Nathaniel Barnwell, Beaufort Dist., 1 Feb 1801; Francis H. Stuart; H. B. Fuller, wit.; Thomas Fuller and Thomas Fuller Jr., trustees. Mar Set 7: 236-238

Maxwell, Robert of Charleston, merchant, & wife Mary, 26 March 1805; Miss Eliza Huxham, trustee; L. Ogier, Thomas Ogier, wit. Mar Set 4: 544-548

Maybank, David of St. Thomas Parish, planter & wife Mary, daughter of Benjamin Simons, 1 March 1804; Thomas Karwon, John Julius Pringle, Isaac Edwards, trustees; John Cort, R. Dorrill, Wm. G. Faber, wit. Mar Set 5: 228-237

Mayrant, John Jr. of Sumter Dist., & Maria P. Rees, of same, spinster, 11 May 1813; William J. Rees, Orlando S. Rees, John B. Miller, John Potts, trustees; Stephen Ford, Jos. J. Singleton, X. J. Bracey, wit. Mar Set 6: 353-358

Mayrant, John Junr, attorney at law, & Maria P. Rees, spinster, Sumter Dist., 11 May 1814; William J. Rees, Orlando S. Rees, John B. Miller, John Potts, trustees; Stephen Ford, Jos. J. Singleton, A. J. Bracey, wit. Misc Rec C, pp. 117-123

Mays, James & Miss Elizabeth Bouchanneau, 20 Oct 1819 in Charleston. St Phil PR

Mazyck, James & Nancy Mosely (people of color), 16 Dec 1819 at Georgetown. Pr Geo Winyaw

Means, Robert of Charleston, Esqr., & Mary Hudson Barnwell, eldest daughter of Hon. John Barnwell, late of Beaufort decd., 19 June 1805; John Gibbes Barnwell, Edward Barnwell, Robert Barnwell, of Beaufort, Esqrs., trustees; James H. Cuthbert, Tho Deveaux, wit. Mar Set 5: 73-79

Medling, Michael & Catharine Jennings, 7 Jan 1806. Moses Waddel

Menicken, John Anthony & Elisabeth Gates, 2 March 1809. St Matthews Luth Ch

Menudet, Jean Baptiste Gabriel & Louise Charlotte Amelie Carendeffox, ___ Feb 1811. St Mary's RC

Metz, Daniel, son of John Metz, & Elizabeth Coogle, 8 June 1815. St Michaels Luth Ch

Mey, Charles & Jane Teasdale, 11 Dec 1813, in Charleston. St Phil PR

Meyniac, Pierre Jacques Francois & Marie Rose Dastas, 9 Feb 1820. St Mary's RC

Michel, Gabriel Sebastien & Marie Louise Chadirac Cournand, 29 Nov 1812. St Mary's RC

Michel, William, doctor of physic, & Eugenia A. Fraser of Charleston, under age of 21, 15 Dec 1820; Peter Orelli & Eugenia Orelli, her guardians; John Michel, Michel L'aine, wit. Mar Set 8: 191-196

Mickle, Joseph of Camden, merchant, & Martha Belton, daughter of John Belton decd., 16 Aug 1802; Abraham Belton of Wateree River, Kershaw Dist., & Robert Mickle, of Camden, merchant, trustees; Thomas Dinkins, Rebecca Mickle, wit. Misc Rec B, pp. 180-183

Middleton, Henry A. & Hariet Kinloch, 20 Jan 1819 at Kensington, near G. T. Pr Geo Winyaw

Miles, George & Mrs. Mary Riley, free colored persons, 20 April 1818 in Charleston. St Phil PR

Miles, Jonathan, son of William Miles, Newberry Dist., S. C., & Mary Pearson, daughter of Enoch Pearson decd., 2 July 1801. Bush R MM

Millar, Daniel & Miss Eliza Love, 24 Dec 1817 in Charleston. St Phil PR

Millar, John and Mary Clark, 3 Oct 1808, William Clark, surety. York Pro 66/3123

Miller, David & Catherine Kohler, 24 Feb 1814, in Charleston. St Phil PR

Miller, John Blount & Mary Elizabeth Murrell, 17 July 1808 in Stateburg, S. C. John Blount Miller Diary, p. 62

Miller, John C. & wife Ann Juliana, daughter of Joseph Legare Jr., late of Christ Church Parish, decd., 11 Jan 1819; John Daniel Legare, trustee; John C. Buckmyer, H. C. McLeod, wit. Mar Set 7: 328-333

Miller, William & Catherine Bennett, 17 April 1813, in Charleston. St Phil PR

Milligan, Andrew & Sarah Stedman, 3 Jan 1805. Moses Waddel

Mills, Andrew & Anna Mills, 9 Nov 1809. Bryan Journal

Mills, John, son of John Mills, Newberry Dist., & Phebe
McDonald, daughter of William McDonald decd., 5 Feb
1801. Bush R MM

Mills, William & Betsy Sutherland, 4 March 1806. Moses
Waddel

Minis, Isaac of Savannah, Georgia & Dinah Cohen, daughter
of Solomon Cohen of Georgetown, 11 Dec 1803; Levi Myers,
physician, of Georgetown, trustee; Moses Myers, J. C.
Moses, wit. Mar Set 4: 335-336

Milon, Pierre Solivor & Caroline Elizabethe Francoise
Perone, 12 June 1820. St Mary's RC

Mitchell, James of Charleston, pump-maker, & Rebecca
Player, of Charleston, spinster, to Rev. William
Capers, 4 Dec 1811. Chaston ML

Mitchell, James D., attorney at law, & Amelia Dorothy V.
Waring, daughter of Thomas Waring Sr., 27 Feb 1809;
William Stevens Smith, trustee; Hess M. Waring,
Horatio Smith Waring, wit. Mar Set 5: 467-469

Mitchell, John Hinckley of Charleston, & Elizabeth Chanler, 25 May 1813; Christian Muldrup Logan, trustee;
John U. Mitchell, Thos. C. Marshall, wit. Mar Set 6:
239-240

Mitchell, John H. & Elizabeth Chanler, 26 May 1813, in
Charleston. St Phil PR

Mitchell, Matthew Pope & Miss Ann Eliza Brown, 13 Jan
1820 in Charleston. St Phil PR

Mitchell, Peter, of Savannah, merchant & Carolina Susan
Putnam of Charleston, spinster, 5 Feb 1816. Chaston
Pro J

Mitchell, Peter & Miss Susan Caroline Putnam, 5 Feb 1816,
in Charleston. St Phil PR

Mitchell, Thomas & Charlotte Mitchell, spinster, ____ 1803;
Samuel Wragg, Thomas Rothmahler Mitchell, trustees;
Job Smith, wit. Mar Set 4: 292-296

Mitchell, Thomas C. and Miss Sarah Anderson, 4 June 1817
in Charleston. St Phil PR

Mitchell, William Boone, & Miss Dorothy S. Richardson, 12
June 1810, in St. Mark's Parish. St Phil PR

Moles, James of Charleston & Margaret Shields, 29 June
1805; William Pritchard Jr., trustee; Wm McCormick,
wit. Mar Set 5: 111-112

Montadon, Henry & Marguerite Helena Devixque, 29 Dec 1818.
St Mary's RC

Montandou, Auguste, "Marchand orloger," legitimate son of
Pierre Henry Montandou and Mariane nee Mathei, native
of Switzerland, aged 33 years, and Margueritte Helena
Devizque, legitimate daughter of Domonique Devixque
and his wife Genevieve Eleanore Renaud, native of St.
Donimgo, aged 26 years, 29 Dec 1818; P. C. Martinet,
Dque. Diron., P. Obagnue, H. Fourgiand, wit. (Original
in French). Mar Set 8: 53-54

Montesquieu & Francoise Reigne, 1 Sept 1816. St Mary's RC

Montgomery, Benjamin R. Dr., & Eliza Nichols, 10 April
1805. Moses Waddel

Montgomery, Benjn R. Rev. & Ann Dunlap, 11 Feb 1808.
Moses Waddel

Mood, Peter, of Charleston, Mariner, & Ann Whipple, of
Charleston, widow, to Rev. James D. Simons, 28 Oct
1809. Chaston ML

Moore, Burgess of Charleston Dist., & Ann Godfrey, widow
of John Godfrey decd., 13 Feb 1804; James Richbourg,
trustee; Henry Richbourg Senr., Robert Crosson, James
Courtonne, wit. Mar Set 4: 361-363

Moore, James of Charleston, house-carpenter, & Elizabeth
Belser, of Charleston, spinster, to Rev. Charles Faber,
27 April 1809. Chaston ML

Moore, Michael, of Columbia, Richland Dist., & Rebecca
Lunsford, 28 May 1803; Robert Stark, & Simon Taylor,
trustees; Geo Wade, David E. Dunlap, wit. Misc Rec
B, pp. 239-243

Moorman, Tarlton, son of Thomas & Susannah Moorman, Rich-
mond Co., N. C., & Hannah Way, daughter of William &
Abigail, Marlborough Dist., S.C., 26 Nov 1807. Piney
Grove MM

Moorman, Uriah, son of Zachariah & Mary Moorman, Marlborough Dist., S. C., & Hannah Mendenhall, daughter of
Stephen & Elizabeth Mendenhall, Richmond Co., N. C.,
20 Nov 1806. Piney Grove MM

Moors, Thos & Miss Milecent Caroline Limehouse, 16 Feb
1817 in Charleston. St Phil PR

Moragne, Francis & Susan Bouchillon, 1 June 1809. Moses
Waddel

Moragne, Francis & Jane Taylor, 14 Nov 1815. Moses Waddel

Mordecai, Goodman & Jane Cohen, 7 Nov 1808; Alexander
    Solomons, step-father of sd. Jane Cohen; Mordecai Lyon,
    Joseph Moses, Samuel Simons, trustees; L. Lawn, Isaac
    Emanuel, wit. Mar Set 5: 410-413

Morgan, William, & Elizabeth Lott, both of Chester Dist.,
    10 June 1819; Samuel McCreary, John Bishop, wit. Misc
    Rec D, pp. 167-168

Moriarty, Maurice, of Charleston, gentleman, & Jane Brady
    of Charleston, widow, 24 Dec 1812; license to Dr.
    William Best. Chaston Pro J

Mork, James & Elizabeth S. Course, 21 April 1814 in
    Georgetown, S. C. St Phil PR

Morland, William-Bennett of Charleston, shoe-maker, &
    Sarah Witter, of Charleston, spinster, to Rev. William
    Capers, 12 March 1811. Chaston ML

Morman, Edward, son of Zachariah & Mary Morman (Moorman),
    Marlborough Co., S. C., & Mary Thomas, daughter of
    Lewis & Agness Thomas, Richmond Co., N. C., 8 May 1800.
    Piney Grove MM

Morris, Harvey & Miss Melicent Alice Jones, 5 Nov 1818 in
    Charleston. St Phil PR

Morris, Henry & Melliscent Alice Jones, spinster, of
    Charleston, 4 Nov 1818; Henry Alexander DeSaussure,
    trustee; Mary Jones, Thos Boone, wit. Mar Set 7:
    309-315

Morris, Matthew, & Julina Cottingham, 26 March 1808,
    married by Rev. Mr. Robert Thomas. Marlboro Pro
    Journal

Morrison, James, of Charleston, cooper, & Jane Douglas
    Miller, of Charleston, spinster, 27 Jan 1810. Chaston
    ML

Morrison, Peter & Christianna Friday, persons of color,
    21 Oct 1819 in Charleston. St Phil PR

Morrison, Robert of St. Bartholomew's Parish, Colleton
    Dist., storekeeper, & Mary A. Hamilton, daughter of
    James Hamilton, __ July 1810; James Stevens, planter,
    trustee. Mar Set 5: 549-551

Morrison, Samuel I. & Miss Eliza Riley, 8 March 1815 in
    Charleston. St Phil PR

Mosely, Henry & Jane McKinly, 28 June 1810. Moses Waddel

Morrow, John & Jane Spence, 24 Oct 1810. Moses Waddel

Mosely, Joseph & Susan Wideman, 23 Dec 1818. Moses Waddel

Mosely, Richd & Mary Montagu, 9 March 1809. Moses Waddel

Moses, Isaac C. of Charleston, & Hannah, daughter of Marks and Rachel Lazarus, 1 Nov 1802; Solomon Cohen of Georgetown, trustee; P. Cohen, Myer Moses, Jacob J. Cohen, wit. Mar Set 4: 268-270

Moses, Simon of Charleston & Esther Simons, daughter of Montague Simons of Jacksonborough, merchant, 5 April 1804; Saul Simons, Sampson Simons, trustees; Chs. Prince, Samuel Simons, wit. Mar Set 4: 401-405

Mosimann, Jacob & Cidalise Escalon, 29 April 1816. St Mary's RC

Moss, Henry A., gentleman & Ann Goodbi Veitch, widow of William Veitch, 7 Sept 1813; A. Buyck, trustee; Jas. Dellet, H. Chanson, A. B. Dulany, wit. Mar Set 6: 268-271

Motta, Judah Arrias, formerly of the Island of Cuzracoa, now of Charleston, & Sarah D'Azevido, daughter of Isaac D'Azevido, 28 May 1804; Rev. Abraham Azuby, Aaron Moise, Aaron Lopez, trustees; E. D. L. Motta, Solomon Hyems, wit. Mar Set 4: 376-380

Moultrie, James of Charleston, physician, & Sarah Louisa Shrewsbury, daughter of Stephen Shrewsbury, decd., 11 Nov 1818; Francis Dickinson, trustee; Charles W. D'Oyley, Thos. Akin, wit. Mar Set 7: 321-328

Mouzon, Charles of Charleston, & Susanna McClellan, 13 May 1802; Thomas Wm Carne, trustee; George Rechon, Ann R. McClellan, wit. Mar Set 4: 206-209

Mouzon, Charles & Miss Mary Lingard Wallis, 4 July 1810. St Phil PR

Muller, Albert A. the Revd. & Miss Martha Frances Rivers, 12 Nov 1817 in St. Philip's Church. St Phil PR

Mullin, Patrick & Barbara Laird, 27 Nov 1817. Moses Waddel

Muncrief, John & Sarah Clarke Schepeler, 26 May 1801; William Clement, trustee; David Johnston, John M. Clement, wit. Mar Set 4: 65-66

Munnerlyn, Charles & Hannah Shackelford, 13 May 1819 at Georgetown. Pr Geo Winyaw

Murph, Henry & Rosina Stoutenmyer, 28 April 1805. St Matthews Luth Ch

Murph, Rudolph & Jane Stoutenmyer, 7 Dec 1802. St Matthews Luth Ch

Murray, John & Bridget Farrah, 5 Feb 1820. St Mary's RC

Murrell, John Jonah of Christ Church Parish, planter, & wife Martha, daughter of William Hall of Charleston, 27 Jan 1800; Thomas Hall, trustee; Thos Hinds, James Jervey, wit. Mar Set 3, pp. 438-440

Myers, David, & Elisabeth Burkett, 5 June 1804. St Matthews Luth Ch

Myers, John F. of St. Bartholomew's Parish, & Sarah Dyzell of same, 5 Dec 1818; Arthur Hughes, trustee; Anne M. Baker, Henry U. May, wit. Mar Set 8: 9-11

Myers, Moses of Georgetown, & Miss Hannah Polock, sister of Isaac Polock, 17 Nov 1801; Dr. Levi Myers & Isaac Polock, trustees; W. M. Duncanson, John Stewart, wit. Mar Set 4: 177-180

Neal, John & Mrs. Sarah Eaves, both of Chester Dist., 21 Aug 1811; Stephen Neal, Saml McCreary, Jno McCrary, wit. Misc Rec C, pp. 324-325

Neely, Saml. & Jean Black, 6 May 1801, Samuel Williamson, surety. York Pro 66/3120

Neguin, John James of Charleston, & Elizabeth Shroudy, widow, 4 April 1800; Jacob Eckhard, Dr. P. J. More, Saml Dickinson, wit. Mar Set 4: 40

Neigle, William of North Carolina and Mary Ann Bigger, 13 Jan 1812. Moses Bigger of York Dist., surety. York Pro 66/3130

Nelson, slave of Mr. H. A. Desaussure & Sylvia Lee, a free person of color, 11 Nov 1819 in Charleston. St Phil PR

Nelson, Christopher & Johanna Maria Hillgendorf, 26 Jan 1814, in Charleston. St Phil PR

Netles, Wm & Caty Holman, 26 Dec 1819. Bryan Journal

Nettles, Wm & Sarah Pillons(?), 4 May 1820. Bryan Journal

Nettles, Zach & Ann Benton, 15 Aug 1816. Bryan Journal

Newby, John N. & Lucy Bickly, 17 June 1801. Moses Waddel

Newson, James & Miss Rachel Port Davis, 7 June 1813.
Marion ML

Newton, Giles, & Elizabeth Smith, to Rev. Robert Purnell,
11 June 1807. Marlboro ML

Newton, William, & Hanna Adams of Marlboro, to Rev. Wm.
Bennett, 25 July 1812. Marlboro ML

Nichols, Jacob & Mary Dubart, 17 Feb 1820. Drehr Journal

Nichols, James & Ann Hollingsworth, Newberry Dist., S. C.,
9 July 1801. Bush R MM

Nicks, Joseph Dewitt & Elizabeth Fair, widow of Richard
Fair, boot and shoe maker, of Charleston, decd., 29
Dec 1818; Dr. Isaac Johnson & James C. Martindale,
Esqr., trustees; Edgar W. Charles, Jno Grigg, wit.
Mar Set 7: 318-321

Niderburgh, Simon N. of Charleston, physician, & Mary
Reynolds, widow, 19 March 1805; Malcolm McKay, grocer,
trustee; John Reid, Alexr Corrie, wit. Mar Set 4:
530-536

Noble, Patrick & Elizabeth Pickens, 5 Sept 1816. Moses
Waddel

Noldens, Piere & Mary Elizabeth Vion, 22 Aug 1804; Charles
Choinard, trustee; Lewis Monnar, wit. Mar Set 4: 438-
441

Normann, George A. & Miss Eliza Jones, 27 April 1815 in
Charleston. St Phil PR

Norris, John & Catharine Howard, 12 July 1804. Moses
Waddel

North, Edward Washington of Liberty County, & Jane Caroline Parker, widow of Ferguson Parker, planter, decd.,
10 March 1802; John Gough, trustee; John Laurens North,
Roger S. Gough, wit. Mar Set 5: 90-93

North, John Laurens & Eliza Elliott Drayton, daughter of
Glen Drayton Esqr., decd., 28 Dec 1805; Hon. John F.
Grimke, trustee; Glen Drayton, Henry Foster, wit.
Mar Set 5: 141-145

Northrup, Amos Bird of Charleston, & Claudia Margaret
Bellinger, daughter of John Bellinger of Colleton Dist.,
decd., 25 April 1809; Samuel Bird Northrup, John S.
Bellinger, trustees; Elianor Bellinger, Andrew Fowler,
wit. Mar Set 6: 175-177

Norwood, Nathaniel & Charlotte Bugg, 24 July 1811. Moses Waddel

Oakford, Aaron of State of Pennsylvania, & Mary McGillivray of Charleston, 3 March 1804; Alexander H. McGillivray, trustee; E. Russell, Eliza Chanler, wit. Mar Set 4: 372-376

Oates, John of St. Paul's Parish, & Hannah Tims, widow, of Charleston, 21 March 1805; John B. Hext, trustee; Henry Fickling, John Girardeau Senr., Benj. R. Porter, wit. Mar Set 5: 243-246

OBrien, Richd. & Jane Lewis, 21 March 1805. Bryan Journal

Oconnor, Patrick & Elizabeth Byrnes, 17 Oct 1820; Grace Doyle, trustee; H. McCaffrey, Mary Ann Kilreay, wit. Mar Set 8: 214-215

O'Connor, T. & Elizabeth Byrnes, 17 Oct 1820. St Mary's RC

Odam, John & Eliza Cain, 8 April 1819. Moses Waddel

O'Hanlon, Terence & Miss Eliza Ann Brown, 4 Aug 1816 in Charleston. St Phil PR

OHara, Arthur & Mary Jane Mazyck, granddaughter of Thomas Young, granddaughter of Benjamin Mazyck, and daughter of Stephen Mazyck, 4 May 1820; Peter J. Shand, John P. Elfe, wit.; Isaac M. Wilson, trustee. Mar Set 8: 125-133

Olds, James & Lucy Banks, 27 April 1819. Moses Waddel

Oliver, Charles & Martha Green, 29 Sept 1814, Richland Dist., Robert E. Russell, Harrit Green, wit. Misc Rec C, pp. 155-156

Oliver, Dyonisius & Jane Clark, 1 April 1804. Moses Waddel

Oliver, James of Charleston, bricklayer, & Elizabeth Limehouse, spinster, 3 Nov 1801; Robert Limehouse, trustee; John Wm. Johnston, Maria D. Umimsetter, wit. Mar Set 4: 137-141

Oliver, John & Sarah Harris, 18 Dec 1816. Moses Waddel

Oliver, Peter of St. John's Parish, Esqr., & Mary Greenland of St. Stephen's Parish, single woman, 14 March 1801; Robert McKelvey of St. John's Parish, and John Couturier, of St. Stephen's Parish, trustees; John Oliver, Saml Axson, wit. Mar Set 4: 30-33

Oliver, Peter, & Mrs. Amelia L. Addison, 31 Jan 1811, in
St. Philip's Church. St Phil PR

Oneale, Charles of Charleston, merchant, and wife Mary,
17 Nov 1805; Archibald Pagan, trustee; Wm Walton, Saml
W. Smith, wit. Mar Set 5: 187-191

O'Neall, Thomas & Sarah, daughter of Robert Evans decd.,
Newberry Co., S. C., 1 Jan 1800. Bush R MM

Osman, George & Mrs. Ryser, 21 Feb 1811. St Matthews
Luth Ch

Osman, George & Margeret Stoutenmyer, 18 March 1813. St
Matthews Luth Ch

Ossard, Pierre, son of Pierre Ossard and Marie Imbert,
born in Monsegur, Dept. of Gironde, France, & Cather-
ine Babin, minor daughter of Pierre Babin and Catherine
Blandin et Anger, widow Babin, born in Mare, Dept. of
L'Oust, St. Domingo; 25 April 1801; Michel Frontz &
Antoine Mariot, wit. (original in French, translated
BHH). Mar Set 4: 38-40

Oswald, David, of Charleston, taylor, and Elizabeth Oliphant, of the same place, spinster, 18 April 1801. St
Phil PR

Otis, Joseph Junior of Charleston, factor, & Jane Munroe,
of Charleston, spinster, to Rev. Richd. Furman, 10 Apr
1810. Chaston ML

Owen, free man of color, & Margaret, slave of Mrs. Williams, 25 May 1820, Radcliffeborough. St Phil PR

Padgett, Samuel & Margaret Goodwin, 10 Dec 1811. Bryan
Journal

Pagels, Christian of Charleston, grocer, & Mary Adams of
Charleston, spinster, to Rev. William Percy, 27 March
1809. Chaston ML

Palmer, George & Rachel Tannehill, 21 Jan 1808. Moses
Waddel

Palmer, Justice & Miss Rachael Souvorris, 19 July 1819
in Charleston. St Phil PR

Parker, Isaac, house-carpenter, & Mary Milligan, of the
same place, 20 July 1800. St Phil PR

Parker, John & Emily Rutledge, 16 April 1812, in Charleston, by Rev. Mr. Fowler. St Phil PR

Parker, Thomas, son of Elisha & Elizabeth Parker, Richmond Co., N. C., & Anne Peele, daughter of Passco & Tabbitha Peele, Richmond Co., N. C., 3 March 1803. Piney Grove MM

Parker, Thomas Junr & Miss Eleanor Legare Frost, 7 Dec 1816 in Charleston. St Phil PR

Parkinson, James & _____ Mary Joy, 17 March 1816, in Charleston. St Phil PR

Parmele, John. of Charleston, shipwright, and Ann Snyder, of the same place, widow, 6 Apr 1802. St Phil PR

Parnand, Jean Alessandro & Marie Wiss, 23 May 1815. St Mary's RC

Pate, Thorogood of Richmond Co., N. C., & Frances Bright, of Marlboro, to Rev. Wm. Bennett, 17 Jan 1807. Marlboro ML

Patrick, Philip of Charleston & Sarah Branford, daughter of Tobias Cambridge, decd., 22 Nov 1820; James Hamilton Junr of Charleston, attorney trustee; S. W. Moore, W. G. Benson, G. B. Ribley, wit. Mar Set 8: 188-191

Patterson, David Capt., and Ann Halliday, 1 Jan 1801. St Phil PR

Patterson, William & Caroline Young, 30 March 1804. Moses Waddel

Paul, slave of Mrs. Wigfall & Susan, a free colored woman, 3 Sept 1816 in Charleston. St Phil PR

Peake, John S. of Charleston & Jane Ewing, eldest daughter of Adam Ewing, merchant, decd., 8 March 1811; James Ewing, Robert W. Ewing, trustees; Agnes B. Johnston, Jno D. Heath, wit. Mar Set 6: 29-33

Pearce, Richard of Charleston, merchant, & Harriet Petsch, of Charleston, spinster, 5 Jan 1813; license to Mr. James D. Simons. Chaston Pro J

Pearce, Richard & Miss Harriet Petsch, 5 Jan 1813 in Charleston. St Phil PR

Pearce, Thomas of Charleston, gentleman, & Ann Lucas, of Charleston, spinster, 12 May 1810. Chaston ML

Pearson, Davis M. of Orangeburg District & Miss Hope Lord Jones, sister of Bruce Jones, 25 June 1819; Sanders Glover, William Murrow, wit. Mar Set 8: 51-52

Pearson, Robert, & Charity Gilbreath, daughter of John
Gilbreath (Galbreath), Newberry Dist., S. C., 6 Dec
1804. Bush R MM

Pearson, Thomas, son of Thomas, Newberry Dist., & Olive
Russell, 9 April 1801. Bush R MM

Peay, Austin F. & Mary English, 4 Jan 1801. Kershaw
Diary

Pebarte, Jean & Marie Madelene Gilbert, 3 Jan 1809. St
Mary's RC

Pendarvis, Josiah of St. George's Parish, Colleton Dist.,
planter, & Ann Rumph, of same, 8 May 1817; Joseph
Koger, trustee; Daniel Sheeder, Isaac Murray, wit.
Mar Set 7: 208-209

Pegues, Christopher B. & Elizar H. Evans, to Rev. Joshua
Lewis, 28 Oct 1811. Marlboro ML

Pegues, James & Sarah Godfrey, to Rev. Joshua Lewis, 23
Dec 1807. Marlboro ML

Pepper, Daniel of Beaufort Dist., & Lydia C. White of
St. Peter's Parish, widow, 26 March 1812; John Cooper
of Purisburg, John Shaw of Savannah, Ga., trustees;
Thos Hardee, Margaret Buche, wit. Mar Set 6: 139-141

Pepper, John of Christ Church Parish, & Ann McDowell, of
St. Thomas Parish, spinster, 2 July 1801; Thos Jones,
Francis Hamlin, wit. Mar Set 4: 78-79

Perdergrass, Conelly & Lydia Ratten, 7 June 1811. St
Mary's RC

Perdriau, John & Ann Michau, daughter of Paul Michau,
decd., 30 Aug 1814; Samuel Perdriau, Benjamin Guerry,
trustees; Alexr Michau, Dorothy Michar, Elizabeth
Guerry, wit. Wmbg DB B, pp. 143-146

Perdriau, Peter, carpenter, & Isabella Benoit Lacombe,
widow, 21 Aug 1812; Dr. Stephen Lacombe, trustee; John
Sharp, William Ruberry, wit. Mar Set 6: 148-150

Perdriau, Peter of Charleston, carpenter & Isabella Benoit Lacombe, of Charleston, widow, 28 Nov 1812; Dr.
Stephen Lacombe, trustee; John Sharp, William Ruberry,
wit. Mar Set 6: 155-156

Perrin, William & Susannah Callum, __ Nov 1803. Moses
Waddel

Perry, Edward D. & Miss Rachel G. Carroll, 10 Nov 1818 on
Charleston Neck. St Phil PR

SOUTH CAROLINA MARRIAGES 1800-1820

Perry, Fabricus of St. Paul's Parish, & Mary Tranquil
    Scott, of same, 20 May 1816; Henry Smith Poyas, of St.
    James Parish, Goose Creek, trustee; Joseph H. Waring,
    Joseph J. Waring, Ann Ball Scott, wit. Mar Set 7: 68-
    70

Perry, Peter & Joanna Beze, __ July 1811. St Mary's RC

Peter, a slave of Thomas Pinckney and Charlotte, a slave
    of Benjm Elliott, 17 March 1816, in Charleston. St
    Phil PR

Peter, Francis, slave of Mrs. Cordes Prioleau, & Clarissa
    Crawley (free person of color), both baptized members
    of St. Philip's church, 14 May 1812, in Charleston.
    St Phil PR

Peterson, Charles & Effie Brown, 10 Feb 1820; license
    directed to Revd. Daniel McKay. Marion ML

Peterson, John Edward of St. George's Parish, Dorchester,
    & Margaret Umback, late Margaret Keckley, 8 June 1811;
    Lewis Poppenheim of St. James Parish, Goosecreek,
    trustee; Chas. Frish, John Strohecker, wit. Mar Set
    6: 39-41

Petigru, James L. & Jane Amelia Postell, Abbeville Dist.,
    22 Aug 1816; James Postell Jr. & wife Jane, trustees;
    M. Waddel, Jas Postell, wit. Mar Set 7: 89

Petigru, James L. & Jane Postell, 22 Aug 1816. Moses
    Waddel

Petigrue, Robert H. of Savannah, Ga., & Eliza E. Mongin,
    of South Carolina, daughter of William Mongin, decd.,
    21 Dec 1815; Daniel William Mongin, John Shellman,
    trustees; John D. Mongin, Geo. Schley, wit. Mar Set
    7: 28-30

Peyton, Henry O. Violetta Wyatt, 23 Nov 1803; Thomas
    Denny, trustee; Andrew Smylie, Wm Aiken, wit. Mar
    Set 4: 390-395

Pezant, Pierre & Rosalie Pellissier, 19 Aug 1809. St
    Mary's RC

Phelan, Edward & Esther Demsy, 31 May 1818. St Mary's RC

Phillips, Aaron of Georgetown & Caroline, daughter of
    Marks & Rachel Lazarus, 24 Feb 1807; Isaac C. Moses
    of Charleston, trustee; Lyon Levy, Jacob Cohen, wit.
    Mar Set 5: 283-284

Pickens, William & Margaret Harris, 27 Nov 1806. Moses
    Waddel

93

Pinckney, Charles Cotesworth & Phoebe Caroline Elliott, 1 May 1811. St Hel PR

Pinckney, Charles Cotesworth & wife Caroline Phoebe, of Charleston, 31 Dec 1816; Phoebe Elliott, widow, and William Elliott, planter, of Beaufort, trustees; mother & brother of sd. Caroline Phoebe; Mary B. Elliott, Jno A. Joyner, wit. Mar Set 7: 104-106

Pinckney, Henry Laurens & Rebecca P. Elliott, 17 Nov 1814, in Charleston. St Phil PR

Pickton, Charles of City of Charleston, house carpenter, & Elizabeth Byers, daughter of William Byers, and granddaughter of Elizabeth Walker, 18 May 1800; Angus Graham, John Walker, trustees; John Hodgson, Thomas Hicky Pickton, wit. Mar Set 4: 288-291

Pickron, James & Elizabeth Nelson, Richland Dist., 16 May 1804; William Trice, trustee; Reuben Horne, John Surginar, wit. Misc Rec. B, pp. 365-367

Pinckney, Thomas Junr., of Charleston, Esqr., & Eliza Izard, spinster, 27 Dec 1803; William Lowndes, trustee; Mary Izard, Thomas Pinckney, wit. Mar Set 4: 420-427

Player, Joshua of Charleston, merchant, son of Thomas Player of Christ Church Parish, decd., and Charlotte Elizabeth Thomson, spinster, daughter of James Hamden Thomson, decd., 1 Dec 1801; Lewis Trezebant, George Cross Junr, David Jervey, George King White, esqrs., trustees; Charlotte Cross, Mary S. White, Eliza Thomson, wit. Mar Set 4: 115-128

Pledger, William & Miss Mary Ann Dalton, 23 Nov 1819 in Wraggborough. St Phil PR

Pledger, William Henry & Sarah Strother, to Rev. Joshua Lewis, 12 July 1802. Marlboro ML

Plenty, slave of Mr. Cromwell & Mary Ann, slave of Mrs. Brodie, 20 Dec 1814 in Charleston. St Phil PR

Plock, David, of Charleston, physician, & Sarah Sampson, of Charleston, widow, 11 July 1817; license to Revd. Thomas Frost. Chaston Pro J

Plumeau, Jean Francaes & Marguerite Reuscpe, 24 Aug 1816. St Mary's RC

Pogson, Milnard & Henrietta Wragg, sister of Elizabeth and Charlotte Wragg, 6 Feb 1805; Alexr Barin Junr., James Ferguson, wit. Mar Set 4: 490-503

Pogson, Milnard and wife, late Henrietta Wragg, who with
her sisters Elizabeth Wragg and Charlotte Smith were
heirs of their mother Henrietta Wragg, and their brother William Wragg, 23 April 1806; Samuel Wragg, James
Ferguson, trustees; Sarah Pogson, Edward C. Lightwood,
wit. Mar Set 5: 480-493

Poincignon, Peter Anthony, plate worker, & Jeane Conlon,
of the same place, widow, 16 Oct 1802. St Phil PR

Polhill, Thomas Jr. & Judith Rebecca Jaudon, daughter of
Elias Jaudon decd., both of St Peter's Parish, 29
March 1813; James Bourdeaux Jaudon, of same parish,
& James Polhill of Georgia, trustees; Elias G. Jaudon,
Sarah Steele, Sarah Jaudon, Benjamin Jaudon, wit.
Mar Set 6: 218-220

Polk, William and Elizabeth Dodds, 22 July 1803. Thomas
Roach, surety. York Pro 66/3133

Pope, Alexander & Dolly Bibb, 9 Aug 1804. Moses Waddel

Pope, John & Louisa Rembert, 25 Nov 1817. Moses Waddel

Porcher, George of St. John's Parish, Berkley Co., &
Mariann Gendron Gignilliatt, widow, 2 May 1805; John
Palmer Jr. & Joseph Palmer Jr., of St John's Parish,
trustees; Isaac Porcher, William A. Moultrie, wit.
Mar Set 5: 93-95

Porteous, Jno & Mary Fuller, 4 June 1818; Benjamin Fuller,
Thos Fuller Jr., William Fuller, trustees; W. T. Brantly, John G. Barnwell, wit. Mar Set 7: 282-284

Porter, John & Margeret Genoble, 27 Sept 1804. St Matthews Luth Ch

Porter, John & Esther Roomer, 16 Dec 1819, at Georgetown.
Pr Geo Winyaw

Porter, William Lamb of Charleston, merchant, & Ann
Saylor, of Charleston, spinster, 17 Jan 1810. Chaston
ML

Posey, John B. & wife, formerly Elizabeth Screven, Beaufort Dist., 31 July 1815; John Screven of Savannah,
trustee; Thomas E. Screven, Mary B. Proctor, wit.
Mar Set 6: 390-392

Postell, Col. James of St. Luke's Parish, & Mrs. Rachel
Kenney, widow, 22 July 1811; Dr. Edward W. North,
Charles J. Jenkins, trustees; Jane Caroline North,
Martha Stafford, wit. Mar Set 6: 82-84

Postell, Philip-Smith, of St. Bartholomew, planter, to
Sarah Dewees, of Charleston, spinster, 23 Nov 1808, to
Rev. James D. Simons. Chaston ML

Powel, Jacob & Elisabeth Miller, 3 May 1801. St Matthews
Luth Ch

Power, Edward of Charleston & Elizabeth Catharine Wolf
of same, spinster, 19 March 1813; Edward Thwing,
trustee; John Strohecker, G. W. Thwing, wit. Mar Set
6: 277-280

Power, Edward, of Charleston, merchant, & Eliza Catherine
Wolf, of Charleston, spinster, 20 March 1813; license
to Mr. Christian Hanckell. Chaston Pro J

Poyas, Henry Smith, & Miss Elizabeth Ann Scott, 27 May
1811, in St. Paul's Parish. St Phil PR

Poyas, James and Miss Charlotte Bryer Bentham, 27 March
1817 in Charleston. St Phil PR

Poyas, John L. of Charleston & Mrs. Providence G. Adams
Cape, widow, __ Feb 1817; Francis G. Deleisseline,
trustee; James C. Norris, St. John Phillips, wit.
Mar Set 7: 152-155

Poyas, John L. & Mrs. Providence G. A. Cape, 20 Feb 1817
in Charleston. St Phil PR

Prauninger, Leonard of Charleston, butcher, & Elizabeth
Hooper, of Charleston, widow, to Rev. Morse, 6 March
1810. Chaston ML

Prentiss, James Otis of Beaufort, now at Brattleboro,
Windham County, Vermont & Anne Reynolds of St. Helena
Island, now at Brattleboro, afsd., 21 Aug 1812; Jona
Townsend, wit. Mar Set 6: 338-339

Price, Obrien Smith & Miss Elizabeth Hamilton M'Call, 6
March 1817 on Charleston Neck. St Phil PR

Price, William Junr of Charleston, planter, & Eliza
Lothrop, of Charleston, spinster, 28 Jan 1812. Chaston
ML

Price, William Junr & Eliza Lothrop, 30 Jan 1812 in
Charleston. St Phil PR

Primrose, Robert & Elizabeth Hext, daughter of William
Hext, late of St. Paul's Parish, decd., 24 March 1813;
William Somersall, Richard Osborn, trustees; Mary P.
Mills, John M. Maillard, wit. Mar Set 6: 226-228

Primus, a free colored man & Diana, slave of Mr. C. Dupre, 26 May 1816 in Charleston. St Phil PR

Prince, slave of I. Shrewsbury & Daphne, 9 May 1814, in Charleston. St Phil PR

Prince, slave of Wm Johnson Senr & Daphne, slave of Mrs. Bonneau (baptized persons), 14 April 1812, in Charleston. St Phil PR

Prince, John, of Charleston, gentleman, & Elizabeth-Bond Bounetheau, of Charleston, spinster, to Rev. James D. Simons, 4 March 1809. Chaston ML

Prince, Oliver H. Maj. & Mary R. Norman, 15 Aug 1817. Moses Waddel

Pringle, James Reid, Esqr., & Elizabeth Mary McPherson, daughter of Gen. John McPherson decd., & Mrs. Susannah McPherson, 18 March 1807; James E. McPherson, John Julius Pringle, trustees; Hy Inglesbey, Wm. S. Bull, wit. Mar Set 5: 296-302

Pringle, Robert-Alexander of Charleston, gentleman, & Sarah-McKewn Maxwell, of Charleston, spinster, 12 June 1810. Chaston ML

Prioleau, Samuel Jr. & wife Hannah Motte Prioleau, daughter of Major James Hamilton, 21 June 1811; James Hamilton Jr., trustee; A. E. Prioleau, William Lance, wit. Mar Set 6: 46-48

Proctor, George V. of Savannah, Ga., practitioner of physic, & Miss Harriet Houstoun, of same, 15 Feb 1810; James E. Houstoun, Joseph Bryan of State of Georgia, & Stephen K. Proctor of S. C., trustees; Mary A. Houston, Sarah Ann Proctor, wit. Mar Set 6: 230-233

Proctor, Stephen R. of S. C., planter & Miss Mary B. Screven of S. C., spinster, 11 Feb 1813; Dr. George V. Proctor, of Georgia, trustee; William Mazyck, Sarah A. Screven, Amelia S. Screven, wit. Mar Set 6: 233-237

Purdy, Joseph of Charleston, mariner, & Johanna Bessilleau, of the same place, spinster, 5 June 1800. St Phil PR

Pursley, Samuel & Nancy Kennedy, 6 Aug 1812. Moses Waddel

Pyke, William Holmes, of St. Bartholomew's Parish, and wife Elizabeth, 4 April 1806; Thomas Hazel, trustee; James Blocker, Owen Buntin, wit. Mar Set 5: 153-155

Quash, slave of Miss Cripps, & Venus, slave of Dr. Poyas, 16 March 1820 in Charleston. St Phil PR

Quash, Francis D. & Miss Emma Doughty, 6 Jan 1819 in Charleston. St Phil PR

Quash, Robert Hasell, of St. Thomas Parish, planter, & Hannah H. Harleston, of St. John's Berkley, spinster, 16 Nov 1815; license to Revd. Christopher E. Gadsden. Chaston Pro J

Quash, Robert H. & Hannah H. Harleston, 23 Nov 1815 in Charleston. St Phil PR

Quin, James, of Charleston, painter, & Ann Reed, of the same place, widow, 27 Sept 1801. St Phil PR

Quin, Thomas Fitzgerald of Charleston, merchant & Eliza Lesesne, 25 April 1804; Jno Speissegger, trustee; G. Smith, Ann Carr, wit. Mar Set 4: 407-412

Ramsay, John D. of Silver Bluff, Edgefield Dist., & Elizabeth Caroline Leacroft, widow, of St. Luke's Parish, Beaufort Dist., 8 Dec 1814; William D. Martin, trustee; N. T. Martin, Edmund Martin, wit. Mar Set 6: 367-368

Ramsey, Thomas & Mary Davis, 7 Jan 1800. Bryan Journal

Randell, Eliah & Mrs. Frances Watkinson, 11 March 1815 in Charleston. St Phil PR

Rauck, George Steven & Anne Garick, 24 Aug 1806. St Matthews Luth Ch

Ravenel, Stephen & Catharine Mazyck, spinster, 11 Dec 1800. St Phil PR

Raynal, Benjamin & Mariam Castel, 11 Jan 1817. St Mary's RC

Read, John H. of Charleston & Mary Withers, now of Elizabeth Town, New Jersey, but late of Georgetown, 8 July 1811; Robert F. Withers, Francis Withers, of Georgetown, trustees; Willis Wilkinson, E. Wilkinson, wit. Mar Set 6: 57-61

Reas, Philemon Dickenson of Charleston, store-keeper, & Jane Lake, of Charleston, spinster, 10 April 1817; license to Dr. William Percy, Rector of St. Paul's. Chaston Pro J

Recardo, Ralph Isreal, formerly of Amsterdam, but now of Charleston & Sarah Hyams, daughter of Solomon Hyams, 26 May 1807; Rachel Hart, trustee; David Abendanone, M. G. Waage, wit. Mar Set 5: 307-312

Reddick, James & Joanna Carrol, 23 April 1810. Moses
Waddel

Reddick, Thomas & Eliza Carrol, 23 April 1810. Moses
Waddel

Redmond, Matthew & Ann Hogan, 2 Feb 1820. St Mary's RC

Rees, Orlando S. Esquire & Miss Catherine Waties, 6 April
1819 by Rev. Parker Adams. Holy Cross Ch

Refor, Sazer, & Eliza M'Clure, col'd persons, 12 Jan 1814,
in Charleston. St. Phil PR

Rees, Loder-Needham, of Charleston, physician, & Eliza-
beth-Martha-Player Legare, of Christ Church parish,
spinster, to Rev. McCallay, 23 Dec 1808. Chaston ML

Rees, William & Miss Eliza Adamson, 13 May 1801. Kershaw
Diary

Reid, Henry Rev. & Jane Wrainch, 1 May 1810. Moses
Waddel

Reid, William & Mary McCromick, 5 Dec 1816. Moses Waddel

Reilly, George of Charleston, Inn-keeper, & Jane Armstrong,
of Charleston, spinster, to Rev. William Percy, 10
July 1810. Chaston ML

Rembert, Andrew & Margaret Sayre, 11 Feb 1819. Moses
Waddel

Remondo, Pierre, merchant, native of Pietra, 51 years
old, son of Nicolas Remondo, and wife Benedicta Bader,
and Pierette Simone Lege, native of Paris, aged 25
years, daughter of Nicholas Lege, and wife Marie
Louise Flamand. __ Feb 1809; (original in French).
Mar Set 5: 451-453

Remoussin, Arnold & Eleanor Lynah, eldest daughter of Dr.
Edward Lynah, 4 Nov 1817; James Lynah, Edward Thomas
Lynah, brothers of Eleanor, trustees; Arthur M. Parker,
Elizabeth Ryan, wit. Mar Set 7: 209-215

Remoussin, Arnold & Eleanor Lynah, daughter of Edward
Lynah, 8 Dec 1818; James Lynah, Edward Thomas Lynah,
trustees; Arthur M. Parker, Robert Browne, wit.
Mar Set 7: 354-358

Renon, Louis Francois of St. Moril D'anger, Dept. of
Menne & Loire, France, aged 45 years, and Marie Pieron
de Esse in Lorraine, for many years resident in Charleston, aged 43 years, 16 Sept 1819; Sebasten Aimar, J. F.
Plumeau, wit. Mar Set 8: 58-60

Renoir, Louis Francois & Marie Pieron, 18 Sept 1819. St
Mary's RC

Reside, William, cabinet maker, of Charleston, & Mary
Magdaline Clarkson, relict of Alexander Clarkson, decd.,
30 July 1800;Joseph Goultier, Philip Helegas, trustees;
Peter Francis Dubuard, Margret Flinn, wit. Mar Set 3:
476-479

Reynolds, Benjamin & Mary E. Chaplain of St. Helena Island,
10 Aug 1819; Archibald Chaplain, trustee; Eliza Chaplin,
Edwin Chaplin, wit. Mar Set 8: 72-74

Rhode, Christian of Polaski County, Ga. & Barbara Murchey,
of St. Mathews Parish, S. C., widow of William Murchey,
24 Jan 1817; Adam Snell, John Evans, John Way, wit.
Mar Set 7: 199-200

Rhodewetz, John & Barbara Voss, Richland Dist., 27 Apr
1820; John J. Myers, trustee; Joseph Blair, Wm. Baus-
kett, wit. Misc Rec D, pp. 339-341

Ricard , Francis, of Charleston, merchant, & Mrs. Mary
Capdeville, of the same place, widow, 3 Oct 1802.
St Phil PR

Rice, Archebald & Ollive Marrs, 21 Feb 1810. Bryan
Journal

Richard, servant of Mrs. Whitaman, & Sophia, servant of
Mrs. Hall, 5 Dec 1813. St Mary's RC

Richard, slave of P. Smith & Flora, slave of R. Pearce,
6 Jan 1814, in Charleston. St Phil PR

Richard, slave of Mrs. Jane Rutledge & Elsy, slave of
do., 26 Aug 1817 in Charleston. St Phil PR

Richardson, Henry, doctor of Medicine, & Mary Fraser of
Charleston, 27 Oct 1801; Henry Fraser, M. D., of
Dawfuskie & John Cattle Livingston of Dawfuskie, James
Lee of Charleston, trustees; (Mary Fraser, niece of
R. R. Ash, and granddaughter of Sarah Odingsell);
Mary Roupell, Henry Wm. DeSaussure, Rd. Fraser, wit.
Mar Set 4: 105-109

Richardson, John, late of Antigua, but now of South
Carolina, & Sarah Frazer of Charleston, 21 Dec 1802;
James Frazer, M. D., John Cattle Livingston, both of
Dawfuskie, & Henry Richardson, of Charleston, trustees;
Joseph Bullein Cook, R. Watts, wit. Mar Set 4: 245-
249

Richardson, Thomas of Charleston, & Miss Sarah Seabrook, 3 April 1806; Thomas Mills, J. H. Cambridge, wit. Mar Set 5: 257-258

Richardson, William & Sally Allison, 22 Oct 1817. Moses Waddel

Riley, Bernard & Honoria Fiztpatrick, 18 Nov 1819. St Mary's RC

Rivers, Thomas Jr. & Rebecca Chambers, 14 Nov 1804; Joshua Player, Aaron Thompson, trustees; Jas. Fogartie, John S. Rose, wit. Mar Set 7: 216-218

Rivet, Francois & Felicite Claudonsen, 6 Feb 1816. St Mary's RC

Roach, Nash & Elizabeth Ann Govan, Orangeburgh Dist., 24 April 1813; Louisa Chevillette, trustee; Sanders Glover, Geo. E. Salley, wit. Misc Rec F, page 292

Roberts, Rev. John Mitchell, of Claremont Co., minister of the Gospel, & Martha Ann Glover Miller, of same; Capt. William Taylor, of Savannah, trustee. Misc Rec. B, pp. 188-191

Roberts, Rev. Dr. John M. & Martha Ann Glover Miller, 31 Oct 1802, near Stateburg, S. C. John Blount Miller Diary p. 56

Robertson, J. & Betsy Hughes, 7 March 1816. Bryan Journal

Robinson, Robert S., Tavern keeper, of Charleston, and wife Ann, 15 July 1805; Daniel Stewart, painter, trustee; Wm. Campbell, wit. Mar Set 5: 56-59

Robinson, William & Pamela Mosely, 30 Jan 1806. Moses Waddel

Robison, Mathew & Sally Emerson, 3 March 1808. Moses Waddel

Robison, William & Mary Ann Yever Miscally, 22 Nov 1817; Daniel Williams Miscally, trustee; Ann Loper, B. F. Dunkin, wit. Mar Set 7: 218-220

Roch, George Charles & Elisabeth de Bardeleben, 27 March 1808. St Matthews Luth Ch

Rodgers, Samuel of Charleston, & Susannah, his wife, daughter of Amey Baker, and granddaughter of Thomas Legare, 29 Apr 1803; J. Burckmyer, Chas. Elliott, John Legare, wit. Mar Set 4: 284-288

SOUTH CAROLINA MARRIAGES 1800-1820

Rodrigues, Francois Xavier & Catherine Boirot, 2 April
    1816. St Mary's RC

Rogers, Benjamin of Marlborough Dist., & Ann Wickham,
    widow, 4 Sept 1804; license directed to Revd. Thomas
    Humphries. Marion ML

Rogers, John & Barbara Breazeal, 13 June 1810. Moses
    Waddel

Rogers, Peter B. & Mary Moragne, 18 March 1802. Moses
    Waddel

Rogers, Peter B. & Mary Palmer, 6 Nov 1816. Moses
    Waddel

Routan, Pierre Jean Marie & Francis Gooth, 21 Sept 1817.
    St Mary's RC

Roy, John & Magdelen Hair, 16 July 1811. St Matthews
    Luth Ch

Rucker, Joseph & Margaret Speer, 5 March 1812. Moses
    Waddel

Rudd, James of St. James Goose Creek, planter, & Sarah
    Bowman, of St. James Goose Creek, spinster, to Rev.
    William Percy, 11 Feb 1812. Chaston ML

Rumley, Edward & Tobitha Lo--both, both of this district,
    by Sam K. Hodges, 13 July 1817. Georgetown Meth Ch

Rumph, G. H. & Mrs. Francis Veronica Rasdale, widow of
    John W. Rasdale, 21 Aug 1820; Francis Due, trustee;
    Peter Gauff, Francis Good, wit. Mar Set 8: 160-164

Rumph, George of St. Bartholomews Parish, & Jennet Allen,
    daughter of Josiah Allen, 21 May 1804; Thomas V. M.
    Hoff, Jacob Zakhler, wit. Mar Set 4: 363-366

Russ, Samuel & Miss Eliza Frierson, 25 Sept 1817 at Ham-
    stead. St Phil PR

Russell, Jeremiah & Sarah Anderson, by William Capers,
    5 June 1817. Georgetown Meth Ch

Russell, John of Charleston & Rachel Milligan, daughter
    of Joseph Milligan, 20 Jan 1811; Margaret Milligan,
    trustee; Owen Keough, Richd. McCormick, wit. Mar
    Set 6: 52-55

Rutledge, Charles of Charleston, Esqr., & Caroline Smith,
    daughter of Roger Smith, 20 March 1800; Thomas Rhett
    Smith & Frederick Rutledge, trustees; Benj. Burgh Smith,
    Charles Flanagan, Robert Limehouse, wit. Mar Set 3:464-
    467

Rutledge, Charles, M. D., of Charleston, & Caroline Smith
of the same place, 25 March 1800. St Phil PR

Ryan, Peter Thomas, of Charleston, merchant, & Elizabeth
Hall Mortimer, of Charleston, spinster, 21 May 1816;
license to Rt. Rev. Bishop Theodore Dehon. Chaston
Pro J

Sabb, Thomas & Sarah Frances Francklow, 19 July 1808.
St Matthews Luth Ch

Sady, slave of Mr. P. Mooney, & Sarah, slave of Mrs. Williamson, 27 May 1819 in Charleston. St Phil PR

Salomon, Levy of Georgetown, merchant & Sarah Harth, widow
of Leo Harth of Charleston, 21 Jan 1805; Abraham Salomon, Peter Smith, trustees; Abm. Alexander, Ralph
Levy, wit. Mar Set 5: 2-5

Saltus, Francis & Miss Rebecca Bonnell, 26 July 1819 in
Charleston. St Phil PR

Sam, slave of Mrs. Michael Lazarus & Martha, slave of Mrs.
M. A. Mathews, 23 Oct 1817 in Charleston. St Phil PR

Sam, slave of Mrs. Mercier & Mary Ann, slave of Col.
Alston, March 1818 in Charleston. St Phil PR

Sancho, slave of Mrs. E. A. Gadsden & Flora, slave of the
Miss Bowmans, 21 May 1818 in Prince George, Winyaw.
St Phil PR

Sanders, Jesse & Jane Germany, 23 Dec 1800. Moses Waddel

Sanders, Jordan, & Miss Ann Nettles, 10 Oct 1805, by
Rev. Benjamin Mosley. Darl MB

Sandford, John & Charlotte Reigne, 30 Nov 1815. St
Mary's RC

Sante, Angelo, living in Charleston, & Francoise Judeh
Ve. Gilleron, 7 March 1804 (original in French). Mar
Set 4: 336-346

Sanit, Angelo, merchant, native of Bologne, Italy, aged
56, widower, son of Santi de Santi and wife Luci, both
deceased, and Francoise Judith L'Etang, widow Gilleron,
from her first marriage has two living children, and
Henriette Dupont, widow Toxier(?), native of Torbee,
St. Domingo, daughter of Pierre Laurent Dupont, and
wife Francoise Murphi, deceased, aged 50 years, 23 Jan
1812. (document not clear, but Francoise Judith L'Etang
appears to have been the first wife of Angelo Santi;
original in French). Mar Set 6: 130-134

Santz, Angelo & Henrietta Dupont, 26 Jan 1812. St Mary's
RC

Sarles, Nathan & Selah Abraham, both of Linches Creek,
Marion Dist., 18 Jan 1802. Marion ML

Sasportas, Abraham of Charleston, merchant, & Charlotte
Canter, daughter of Jacob Canter, merchant, decd., 31
Dec 1802; Rene Godard, Joshua Canter, trustees. Mar
Set 4: 241-244

Sauerhoffen, Conrad & Elisabeth White, 12 April 1801. St
Matthews Luth Ch

Savage, Saml S. of Big Pee Dee, & Eliza C. Nesbitt, spinster, 7 Aug 1807; license directed to Revd. Mr. William Palmer. Marion ML

Schipman, Harmand Berens & Anna Elisabeth Zweiter, 19
July 1814. St Mary's RC

Schmidt, John Wilson, Practitioner of Physic, & Ursule
Dumont of Charleston, 20 Jan 1810; Peter Ayrault, trus-
tee; James S. Nielson, Richd McCormick Pebarte, wit.
Mar Set 5: 529-540

Scott, Green Hill & Hariot Fleming of Georgetown, widow,
2 June 1808; William Murray, trustee; William Grant,
Samuel C. Smith Jr., wit. Mar Set 5: 406-409

Scott, James & Margaret Hutchison, 20 Oct 1815. Moses
Waddel

Scott, James & Miss Mary Eliza Martin, daughter of Mrs.
Sarah Fowler Martin, 20 May 1818; David Ross, Sarah
A. Martin, wit. Mar Set 7: 301-302

Scott, John & Eleanor Brock, 20 May 1813. Moses Waddel

Scott, Thomas, planter & Eliza Robinson, spinster, both
of Williamsburg District, 15 May 1815; James Burgess,
Saml R. Mouzon, trustees; Duncan Gilchrist, John
Scott Sr., wit. Mar Set 7: 56-57

Scott, William & Mary Millar, __ Nov 1803. Moses Waddel

Scott, William Morgan of Charleston, & Margaret Holmes of
same, widow, 28 Sept 1811; John Everingham, John Ellison, trustees; Samuel Alexander, Rebecca Everingham,
wit. Mar Set 6: 104-106

Scott, William Morgan, of Charleston, merchant, & Margaret Holmes of Charleston, widow, 30 Sept 1811.
Chaston ML

Screven, John of Georgia, and Sarah Ann Proctor of May
River, spinster, 18 March 1812; Joseph Bryan, Stephen
R. Proctor, Charles Harris, esqrs., trustees; Mary
Screven, William B. Johnson, John T. Bolles, wit. Mar
Set 6: 150-153

Screven, Dr. Richard B. & Mary Rhodes, widow of Dr. Nat-
haniel H. Rhodes, 9 Dec 1819; John Rhodes, James
Bowman, trustees; Mary L. Christian, Morton A. Waring,
Susan B. Hamilton, wit. Mar Set 8: 136-139

Seabrook, Benjamin Esqr. of Edisto Island, planter, &
Margaret Jenkins, relict of Isaac Jenkins, Esqr., 27
May 1800; Paul Hamilton, & William C. Meggett, Esqrs.,
trustees; Daniel Jenkins, Jos. J. Murray, wit. Mar
Set 3: 446-448

Seabrook, Gabriel of St. John's Parish, Colleton Dist.,
& Mrs. Ann Campbell, widow of Edward W. Campbell, 20
Nov 1810; Joseph Jinkins, trustee; Benj. Reynolds,
James Laroche, wit. Mar Set 6: 37-39

Sealy, Ezekiel & _____ McClesky, __ Sept 1801. Moses
Waddel

See, William & widow Boozer, 16 Jan 1820. Drehr Journal

Seebra, Shem & Eliza. Scott, 3 March 1809. Bryan Journal

Segistrom, John Gustavus of Charleston, grocer, & Jane
Glaise, 30 March 1808; John Dupuy, Onezime Pillot,
trustees; F. Rivire, J. S. Neilson, wit. Mar Set 5:
385-389

Sellers, Andrew & Magdelen Whetstone, 20 Aug 1803. St
Matthews Luth Ch

Sellers, Andrew & Dorothy Beniger, 18 Oct 1804. St
Matthews Luth Ch

Sellers, Andrew & Mary Brandeburg, 26 Jan 1813. St
Matthews Luth Ch

Sellers, Jacob & Sarah White, 19 Feb 1801. Bryan Journal

Serisier, Louis Arvengas & Sarah Smith, widow, 24 Oct
1800. St Phil PR

Sessions, Joseph & Martha Mary Wilson, 1 Aug 1818 at
Georgetown. Pr Geo Winyaw

Sevier, Alexander, Major, & Miss Jane Bacot, 16 Feb 1815
in Charleston. St Phil PR

Shackelford, John & Mary Godfry, 19 Dec 1820 at Georgetown in Church. Pr Geo Winyaw

Shackelford, John W. of Georgetown, & Eliza S. Tait of
same, 24 April 1816; Joseph Blythe, John Keith, trustees; Thomas Henning, W. Chapman, wit. Mar Set 7:
65-67

Shackelford, John W. & Elizabeth S. Tait, 24 April 1816,
at Georgetown. Pr Geo Winyaw

Shackelford, Richard of Georgetown, & Mary Hutchinson, of
same, widow, 19 Nov 1807; Jeremiah Cuttino, trustee;
Thos Evans, David Cuttino, Peter Cuttino, wit. Mar
Set 5: 376-381

Shackleford, James & Harriet Cowdry, 15 Dec 1814. Moses
Waddel

Shanklin, Thomas & Mrs. Barksdale, 4 Aug 1806. Moses
Waddel

Sharp, John of Charleston, clock-maker, & Elizabeth Doré,
spinster, 3 March 1800. St Phil PR

Sharpe, James of Prince Williams Parish, Beaufort Dist.,
& Mary Fitzgerald, 29 March 1815; James Grayson,
Philip Givens, trustees; John Read, B. Branford,
George Gardnes, wit. Mar Set 6: 374-377

Shaw, Joseph & Mary Calahan, 11 March 1819. Moses Waddel

Shea, Richard & Mrs. Frances Lundquest, 19 March 1815, in
Charleston. St Phil PR

Shearman, George W. of Parish of St. Helena & Elisabeth
Tucker, 3 July 1806; John Jenkins Jr., trustee; J. B.
Cook, John Lugg, wit. Mar Set 8: 166-167

Sherrod, Benjamin & Eliza H. Watkins, 1 Jan 1808. Moses
Waddel

Shields, Samuel B. & Willy H. Glover, 31 March 1808.
Moses Waddel

Shirtliffe, William Lee & Ann Lewis Gibbes, persons of
color, 1 July 1818 in Charleston. St Phil PR

Shoemaker, James & Martha Beall, 16 May 1816. Moses
Waddel

Shoolbred, John G. of Charleston & Emma A. Gibbes, 23 Oct
1820; Joseph S. Gibbes, John Reeves Gibbes, trustees;
Robert Gibbes Jr., James L. Gibbes, wit. Mar Set 8:
170-178

Short, William & Mrs. Charlotte Elliott, 25 Nov 1819 in
    Charleston. St Phil PR

Shubrick, Edward R. & wife Esther Mary, of Georgetown
    District; (no date) proved 8 Dec 1820; Ebenezer Flagg,
    Irvine Shubrick, trustees; P. Trapier, Elias Horry,
    wit. Mar Set 8: 181-183

Shular(?), Conrod & Caty Gable, 22 June 1820. Drehr
    Journal

Shular, John, son of Leonard Shular and wife, Nancey,
    married to the Widow Kleckley, 1801. St Michaels
    Luth Ch

Shular, Thomas, son of Leonard Shular and wife, Nancy,
    married Ann Drehr, 28 April 1812. St Michaels Luth Ch

Sidney, slave of J. D. Simons, & Betsy, slave of Mrs.
    James Cox, 30 April 1814, in Charleston. St Phil PR

Silliman, John H. & Eliza Milligan, 2 Dec 1812. 2d Pres
    Ch

Silva, Domingo & Eleanor Hill, 21 Dec 1818. St Mary's RC

Simmons, Dennis of Parish of St. George Colleton, & Eliz-
    abeth Coveney, widow, of same, 15 June 1815; John
    Simmons, trustee; Esther Simmons, Sarah Holland, Mary
    Nell, wit. Mar Set 6: 406-408

Simmons, Thomas Hayne of Charleston, & Mary Jones Reid,
    24 Feb 1817; Francis Motte, William Edward Hayne,
    trustees; John Ward Mathews, Jno Moore Mathews, wit.
    Mar Set 7: 149-151

Simons, Charles Dewar of Charleston Dist., & Sarah Barks-
    dale, daughter of Thomas Barksdale, Esqr., late of
    Christ Church Parish, decd., 1 Sept 1807; George Ed-
    wards of Beaufort Dist., trustee; Mary Barksdale, Rt.
    Dewar, Sabina Bonneau, wit. Mar Set 5: 347-354

Simons, James & Sarah Tucker Harris, of Charleston,
    spinster, 29 Dec 1800; Tucker Harris, physician, trus-
    tee; Wm Webb, Hyam Solomon, wit. Mar Set 4: 21-25

Simons, James & Sarah Tucker Harris, 30 Dec 1800. St
    Phil PR

Simons, Keating Lewis & wife Ann Cleland Simons, daughter
    of Francis Kinloch, Esqr., __ Jan 1819; Fredk. Rutledge,
    trustee; John Moultrie, Benjn C. Gadsden, wit. Mar
    Set 7: 338-340

Simons, Maurice Junr & Miss Eliza Capers, 4 Sept 1817 on
  Sullivan's Island. St Phil PR

Simons, Maurice & Rachel Elfe, 21 April 1813, in Charleston. St Phil PR

Simons, P. Edward & Miss Catharine M. Patterson, 26 Nov
  1817 in Charleston. St Phil PR

Simons, Sedgwick & Miss Ann Hume, 10 Oct 1815 in Charleston. St Phil PR

Simons, Thomas Grange & Miss Katherine Hume, 19 March
  1815, in Charleston. St Phil PR

Simpson, John & Nancy Glover, 24 Jan 1805. Moses Waddel

Simpson, John & Mrs. Sarah Hunter, 22 Jan 1811; Laurens
  Dist., John Caldwell, trustee; James Brown, John B.
  Kennedy, wit. Misc Rec C, pp. 227-228

Sims, William & Rebekah H. Gray, 7 March 1816. Moses
  Waddel

Sinclair, Alexander, merchant & Margaret Ewing, daughter
  of Adam Ewing, late of Charleston, decd., 23 Jan 1817;
  John S. Peake, trustee; Archd S. Johnston, Michl Peake,
  wit. Mar Set 7: 115-119

Singellton, Benjamin, of Charleston & Elizabeth Ladson of
  St. Paul's Parish, 31 Oct 1816; George Henry Smith,
  Francis Dickinson, trustees; Jane Perry, W. C. Stewart,
  wit. Mar Set 7: 83-88

Singleton, Mr. & Harriet English, 23 Feb 1809. Kershaw
  Diary

Singleton, James & Louisa Belser, 10 March 1814 in Charleston. St Phil PR

Skinner, William and Elizabeth Nolen, 27 March 1804.
  John Mills, surety. York Pro 66/3121

Slaughter, William A. & Martha Collier, 21 Nov 1815.
  Moses Waddel

Smidt, Joannes G. & Ursula Beaumont, 20 Jan 1810. St
  Mary's RC

Smith, Benjamin Burgh of Charleston, Esqr., & Ann Stock,
  of Charleston, spinster, 9 Feb 1804; Thomas Rhett
  Smith, Thomas Stock, John Stock, trustees; Ann A.
  Chiffelle, Chs. Lining, wit. Mar Set 4: 385-390

Smith, Charles & Emeline Eberhard, 2 July 1801. St Matthews Luth Ch

Smith, Frederick, of Charleston, grocer, & Eliza Smith (formerly Eliza Kerr of Charleston, spinster, now his wife); 22 Nov 1802; Thomas Keenan, trustee; Oliver Cromwell, wit. Mar Set 4: 235-237

Smith, G. Henry of St. George's Parish, & Maria Day, of St. Paul's Parish, 23 March 1816; Jeremiah Miles of St. Paul's Parish, trustee; Francis Dickinson, Susan Dickinson, Louisa Shrewsbury, wit. Mar Set 7: 32-35

Smith, John, of Charleston, upholster, & Elizabeth Reynolds, of the same place, widow, 19 Feb 1802. St Phil PR

Smith, John Jr. & Eleanor Brown, 6 March 1810. Marion ML

Smith, Joseph, son of William & Jean Smith, Union Dist., & Elizabeth Comer, daughter of Joseph & Elizabeth, 27 Sept 1804. Cane Cr MM

Smith, Press McPherson of Georgetown, Esqr., & Harriot Lesesne of St. Thomas's, spinster, 24 March 1802; Peter Lesesne, trustee; Caroline Blamyer, William Blamyer, wit. Mar Set 4: 189-192

Smith, Press McPherson, of Charleston, Esqr., & Margaret Cantey of St. Stephen's Parish, spinster, 2 Nov 1820; Samuel Dubose, trustee; Anna H. Thomas, wit. Mar Set 8: 199-201

Smith, Samuel of Georgetown Dist., & Harriet Emma Waring, daughter of Sarah Waring, 10 Feb 1819; Joseph Waties Allston, Davison McDowell, W. W. Trapier, Thomas Carr, trustees; Charles Ann Allston, Esther C. Rothmahler, wit. Mar Set 7: 340-345

Smith, Thomas of Chehaw, planter, & Elizabeth Mary Baker of Charleston, 19 April 1810; Joseph Bennett, trustee; William P. Dove, W. H. Baker, wit. Mar Set 5: 526-529

Smith, Walter of Charleston, mariner & Hester Keenan, widow of Thomas Keenan, 25 Feb 1814; Thomas Winstanley, trustee; James Turnbull, Abraham Jones, wit. Mar Set 6: 303-304

Smith, Walter & Esther Keenan, 29 Feb 1814 in Charleston. St Phil PR

Smith, Whiteford Jr. & Margaret Shand, 31 Oct 1811. 2d Pres Ch

Smith, William & Aminta Gray, 27 July 1815. Moses Waddel

Smith, William Esqr., of the State of New York, & Rosella
B. Torrans, of Charleston, spinster, 12 Dec 1810; Mrs.
E. B. Hatter, Thomas W. Bacot, Hugh Patterson, trustees;
Peter Bacot, Henry H. Bacot, wit. Mar Set 6: 6-11

Smith, William Loughton of Charleston, Counsellor at law,
& Charlotte Wragg of Ashley Baroney, spinster, daughter
of Hon. William Wragg, 18 Dec 1805; Gabriel Manigault,
James Ladson, Nathaniel Heyward, trustees; Henry H.
Bacot, John Simmons, wit. Mar Set 5: 112-130

Smoak, John Daniel & Anna Christena Johnson, 20 April
1802. Bryan Journal

Smoke, Wm & Nancy Crossby, 6 Oct 1811. Bryan Journal

Smylie, Andrew & Susanna Bruce, widow, 8 Oct 1801. St
Phil PR

Smyth, Robert of Abbeville Dist., & Martha Boggs, daughter
of Elizabeth Boggs, widow, 8 Feb 1813; John Pressly,
Jno Devlin, wit. Mar Set 6: 212-213

Snowden, Rev. Mr. Charles B. of St. Stephens Parish, &
Maria Drake of same, spinster, 16 April 1812; Sims
Lequeux, Samuel Dubose of St. John's Parish, trustees;
Christopher E. Gadsden, Francis Peyre, wit. Mar Set
6: 123-125

Snyder, Wm. H. & Ann I. Riley, slaves of Mrs. Harriett
Rutledge, both colored persons, 3 Nov 1814, in Charleston. St Phil PR

Solomon, Israel, formerly of Amsterdam, Holland, now of
Georgetown, & Eleanor Joseph, daughter of Lizar Joseph
of same, 5 May 1814; Abraham Alexander Jr., Abraham
Otolen, trustees; Nathl Coggeshall, Jacob Myers, wit.
Mar Set 6: 323-325

Solomon, Sampson, of Georgetown, formerly of Amsterdam,
province of Holland, & Miss Molcy Joseph, daughter of
Lizar Joseph of Georgetown, 17 Feb 1819; Israel Solomon & Lewin Cohen, trustees; Moses Myers, P. C. Cogg-
shell, wit. Mar Set 8: 1-2

Span, Charles Jr., gentleman & Eleanor Crowley of Charleston, spinster, 16 May 1807; John Horn of Statesborough,
trustee; Wm. Keating, Joshua Reynolds, wit. Mar Set
5: 368-376

Sparrow, James & Ellen Merkle, widow of Frederick Merkle,
7 Oct 1820; Whiteford Smith, trustee; Robert Clark,
Bird Rulby, James Calden, wit. Mar Set 8: 167-170

Spears, George T. of Charleston, factor & Mrs. Caroline
Parker Edwards, of Greenwich, in Christ Church Parish,
(no date, recorded 16 Jan 1817); George Barksdale of
Greenwich and James F. Edwards of Charleston, trustees;
Wm Scott, Sarah P. Scott, wit. Mar Set 7:106-108

Speer, John & Eliza Caldwell, 31 Oct 1807. Moses Waddel

Speer, William & Polly Gill, 3 Dec 1811. Moses Waddel

Spence, Robert & Maria McNeil, 14 June 1810. Moses Waddel

Spencer, Seth & Mrs. Maria James, 21 March 1819 in Charleston. St Phil PR

Spierin, George H. Revd. of Georgetown Dist., & Mary
Elizabeth Tucker, widow of Daniel Tucker, 28 May 1801;
George Heriot, trustee; Will. Heriot, Jno Keith, wit.
Mar Set 4: 69-73

Stanford, David & Sally Upton, _____ 1800. Moses
Waddel

Stevens, _____ B. & Mary Rutledge, 19 Nov 1817. Bryan
Journal

Stevens, Benja. & Rebeckah Davis, 21 March 1805. Bryan
Journal

Stevens, Rubin(?) & Narcissa Rutledge, 17 Oct 1819.
Bryan Journal

Stevens, Wm. & Anna Tiner, 16 Dec 1802. Bryan Journal

Stanton, Samuel, son of Samuel & Mary Stanton, of Ran-
dolph Co., N. C., & Sarah Hollingsworth, daughter of
Isaac & Susannah Hollingsworth, Newberry Dist., S. C.,
2 May 1805. Bush R MM

Stevens, William Smith of Charleston, physician, and wife
Hannah Ashe, widow of Samuel Ashe, late of Charleston,
decd., 14 Jan 1806; Samuel Barksdale Jones, trustee;
Geo R. Logan, wit. Mar Set 5: 165-186

Stewart, Charles of Charleston, barrister, & Adriana
Grant, 10 Sept 1803; William Robert Bull, William
Robertson, Joshua Lockwood, trustees; O Cromwell, Ann
Dawson, wit. Mar Set 4: 526-530

Stewart, Henry slave of Mrs. _____ & Rachel Gadsden, free
person of color, 16 Sept 1819 in Mazyckborough. St
Phil PR

Stewart, John & Jane M. Harris, 19 Dec 1811. Moses
Waddel

Stewart, Robert & Miss Martha Stoll, 12 Nov 1820 in St. Philip's. St Phil PR

Stingley, John & Sally Bernhart, 14 June 1814, by Revd. Paul Henkle. St Michaels Luth Ch

Stock, John Esqr., & Miss Ann Alicia Chiffelle, granddaughter of Thomas Hutchinson Esqr., 22 May 1806; Thomas R. Smith, Thomas P. Chiffelle, Thomas Stock, trustees. Mar Set 5: 339-340

Stokes, Henry & Mary Cannon, 8 Aug 1811. Bryan Journal

Stokes, Richard & Mary A. C. Crayton, 15 Dec 1807. Moses Waddel

Stoutenmyer, Daniel & Magdelen Weis, 9 July 1809. St Matthews Luth Ch

Stoutenmyer, Jacob & Margeret Irick, 26 Nov 1805. St Matthews Luth Ch

Strange, _____ & Mary Huggans, 20 April 1813. Bryan Journal

Street, Joseph & Miss Elvia Gapper, 9 Oct 1820 in Charleston. St Phil PR

Sturgis, Josiah of Charleston, merchant, & Mary Johnston, spinster, daughter of Charles Johnston, decd., 28 Jan 1812; James Macbeth, Doddrige Crocker, trustees; C. Johnston, Anna Johnston, J. S. Lovell, wit. Mar Set 6: 100-104

Sturgis, Josiah of Charleston, merchant, & Mary Johnston of Charleston, spinster, to Rev. John Buchan, 3 Feb 1812. Chaston ML

Sulevan, Daniel & Elenar Robertson, 5 July 1804. Bryan Journal

Sutton, John D. & Sarah Darley, 15 March 1804. Bryan Journal

Swanson, David & Ann Shaw, widow of Archibald Shaw, late of All Saints Parish, who died intestate, 27 March 1801; James Wilson, physician, trustee; Alexander Campbell, Alex McKenzie, wit. Mar Set 4: 36-38

Swinton, James of Charleston & Eliza Bailey, sister of Benjamin Bailey, 16 Nov 1804; H. Swinton, James M. Ward, wit. Mar Set 4: 536-540

Surginer, John & Elizabeth Randol, Richland Dist., 18
    March 1815; Robert Weston, James Adams, trustees; John
    Penny, Ann Penny, Richard Bolan, wit. Misc Rec C, pp.
    171-177

Surls, Beneagy, & Tabitha Low, 25 Oct 1814. Marion ML

Sutherland, William & Margt. Heminger, 25 Sept 1818.
    Moses Waddel

Sutton, John & Miss Elizabeth Albinson, 22 July 1818 in
    Charleston. St Phil PR

Swinderwine, William & Marie Rose Polony, 3 Jan 1815.
    St Mary's RC

Swinney, Darby H. & Martha Wilson, 6 July 1816; Martha
    Smith, John F. Wilson, trustees; Mary A. Burch, Josiah
    J. Evans, wit. Mar Set 7: 70-71

Symonds, Joseph W. Dr. & Jane Calhoun, 9 Sept 1815.
    Moses Waddel

Symonds, William M. & Eliza Jackson, daughter of Thomas
    Jackson, 25 July 1812; John J. Byrd, Peter Thomas, wit.
    Mar Set 6: 420-423

Symonds, William M. & Eliza Jackson, 26 July 1812. 2d
    Pres Ch

Tahan, Joseph of St. Domingo, native of Mortargis in
    France, son of Joseph Tahan & Marie Francoise Boutill-
    ier, and Marie Terassen, widow of Jean Jacques Chartier,
    native of Rochelle, France, 4 June 1801; M. M. Leonard,
    Henry Mussault, Claude Deliol, Henry Hattier, wit.
    (original in French, translated BHH). Mar Set 3: 494-
    497

Taliaferro, Benjn & Martha Watkins, 15 Oct 1807. Moses
    Waddel

Tally, Alexander & Miss Caroline Pinckney, 3 May 1818 in
    Charleston. St Phil PR

Tamarus, Charles Christian of Charleston, & Frances Morin,
    16 Jan 1809; John Thomas, Joseph Beaudrot, trustee;
    Peter Cordier, wit. Mar Set 5: 494-495

Tannehill, Benjn & Agnes Johnson, 6 Dec 1808. Moses
    Waddel

Tarbox, John & Sarah F. Avant, 12 Aug 1819. Georgetown
    Meth Ch

Tart, Enos & Susannah Johnston, spinster, 14 Sept 1807.
Marion ML

Tastet, Pierre Raymond & Jeanne Monicotte, 1 Sept 1810.
St Mary's RC

Tate, Waddy Dr. & Eliza E. Thomson, 14 Jan 1808. Moses
Waddel

Taylor, James & Mary Taylor, 31 Oct 1816. Moses Waddel

Taylor, Josiah of Charleston, factor & Mary Stiles Rivers,
daughter of Jane Elizabeth Dill, widow, 27 Nov 1805;
George Rivers, William McCants of St. Andrew's Parish,
trustee; Jacob Ford, James Mitchell, wit. Mar Set 5:
132-140

Taylor, Thomas & _____ Chapman, 1 Jan 1820. Georgetown
Meth Ch

Taylor, William & Rebekah Corley, 30 Sept 1819. Drehr
Journal

Telfair, Thomas & Margaret Long, 16 March 1809. Moses
Waddel

Tennant, Robert, merchant, & Mary Ann Aitchison, of
Charleston, 14 April 1813; William Russell, Thomas
Denny, physician, trustees; James Dennison, James S.
Neilson, wit. Mar Set 6: 197-201

Terrill, William of Black Mingo & Maryann McClockin, of
Charleston, 15 Dec 1803; Henry Geddes, trustee; W.
Johnston, Wm. Leys, wit. Mar Set 4: 427-432

Tharin, Lewis Senr. of Charleston, gentleman & Eliza
Sophia Cunnington, spinster, daughter of William
Cunnington decd., 22 Nov 1804; William Yeadon, trustee;
E. Hornby, E. W. Weyman, wit. Mar Set 4: 519-526

Theus, Simeon Junr & Miss Susannah Bentham, 11 March 1818
in Charleston. St Phil PR

Theus, William R. of Georgetown, & Elizabeth Love Lenud
of same, daughter of Henry Lenud, late of Claremont
County, decd., 30 Oct 1806; Francis G. Deliesseline,
Henry Laurens Lenud, trustees; Frans. A. Deliesseline,
Aaron Marvin, John S. Cogdell, wit. Mar Set 5: 266-
274

Theving, Edward, of Charleston, house carpenter, &
Margaret Wolf, of the same place, widow, 25 July 1802.
St Phil PR

Thomas, slave of Mr. Johann Williams & Susannah, slave
of Mrs. Campbell, 1 Jan 1815 in Charleston. St Phil PR

Thomas, Benjamin, son of John & Molley Thomas, Marlborough
Dist., S. C., & Ann Moorman, daughter of Zachariah &
Mary Moorman, Marlborough Dist., S. C., 23 Oct 1806.
Piney Grove MM

Thomas, Edward Gibbes of Charleston, physician, & Emily
Wakefield, spinster, 21 Nov 1804; Martha Cannon, Thomas
Doughty, trustees; Em. Logan, Wm. Johnston, wit. Mar
Set 4: 485-489

Thomas, James Esqr., merchant, of Charleston & Mary Magdalene Inglis Clitherall, spinster, 14 Nov 1815; William Lance of Charleston & George Clitherall of North
Carolina, trustees; Geo. Hy. Inglis, Harriet B. Crafts,
wit. Mar Set 7: 7-10

Thomas, Samuel, physician, of Georgetown, & Mary Gaillard,
spinster, of Charleston, 13 Feb 1803; John Gaillard,
Esqr., planter, trustee; Edward Croft, Peyre Gaillard,
wit. Mar Set 4: 250-256

Thomas, Solomon, son of Isaac & Rachel Thomas, Richmond
Co., N. C., & Anna Morris, daughter of Thomas & Sarah
Morris, Marlborough Dist., S. C., 23 April 1812.
Piney Grove MM

Thomas, Stephen & Mary Ann Pressly, 25 April 1811. 2d
Pres Ch

Thomas, Stephen, son of Lewis & Agnes Thomas, Richmond
Co., N. C. & Lilly Dawson, daughter of Daniel & Ann
Dawson, Marlborough Dist., S. C., 21 Jan 1813. Piney
Grove MM

Thomas, William, son of Isaac & Mary Thomas, Laurence
Dist., S. C., & Sarah Pemberton, daughter of Isiah &
Elizabeth Pemberton, both decd., 1 April 1802. Bush
R MM

Thompson, Alexander of Charleston, bricklayer, & Martha
Ann Miller, spinster, daughter of Samuel Miller, house
carpenter, __ Aug 1804; John Palmer, house carpenter,
trustee; Thomas Walker, James Evans, wit. Mar Set 4:
432-438

Thompson, George of Charleston, bricklayer & Ann Margaret
Threadcraft, daughter of Bethel Threadcraft, late of
Charleston, watch maker, __ Jan 1816; John Ralph
Rodgers, ship chandler, trustee; John Rose, John
Tillinghast Jr., wit. Mar Set 6: 426-429

Thompson, Joseph, son of Richard, Padgetts Creek, Union
Dist., & Lydia Randol, daughter of Joseph Randol, 27
Oct 1802. Cane Cr MM

Thompson, Samuel, gentleman, & Elizabeth McRee, spinster,
7 July 1804; license directed to Rev. Philip Kirton.
Marion ML

Thomson, James & Susan Covin, 21 Feb 1811. Moses Waddel

Thomson, Thomas & Eliza Turnbull, 19 Dec 1816. Moses
Waddel

Thornhill, Briant, & Sarah Hutson, __ Jan 1805; Austin
Temple (x), Amos Thornhill, sec; Jas. Holding, wit.
Darl MB

Thurmond, Pleasant of Edgefield Dist., & Sarah Quarles,
15 Dec 1818; William Lomax, trustee; Aaron Tutts,
Susannah Quarles, wit. Misc Rec D, pp. 97-100

Thwing, Edward of Charleston, & Mrs. Margaret Wolf, one
of the children of the sisters of John Eberly (married
25 July 1802); this agreement made 5 Aug 1809; Edmund
Green, trustee; Joseph Finch, wit. Mar Set 5: 470-472

Todd, John & Julia Spencer, __ June 1800. Moses Waddel

Tofel, John of Charleston, confectioner & Angeline English
of same, spinster, 15 May 1808; Jean Baptiste Benoist,
baker, trustee; Joseph Jaban, Francois Duboe, wit.
Mar Set 5: 458-460

Tofel, John & Angelique English, 15 May 1809. St Mary's
RC

Toohey, Michael & Ellen Doyle, 15 Feb 1819. St Mary's RC

Toomer, Joshua of St. Helena, planter, & Mary Elizabeth
Smith, widow of Thomas Smith, 10 Feb 1820; Joseph Ben-
nett of Charleston, attorney, trustee; John Jenkins,
William Myers, wit. Mar Set 8: 99-100

Tootle, Rigdon & Mary Murdick, 13 Dec 1810. Bryan Journal

Torre, Antonio Della of Charleston, merchant, & Margaret
Ann Ryan, of Charleston, spinster, 4 June 1816; license
to Simon Felix Gallagher. Chaston Pro J

Torrey, Capt. William of Charleston, & Ann Prince, of the
same place, spinster, 30 May 1800. St Phil PR

Towers, George W. & Frances Dupont, 17 June 1817; Joseph
Longworth, trustee; Sophia McBride, Jno Crawford, wit.
Mar Set 7: 195-197

Townsend, John R. & Amelia Eliza Waring, daughter of Joseph Waring, late of St. George's Parish, decd., 9 March 1820; Joseph Ioor Waring, of St. Paul's Parish, trustee; John T. Jenkins, Daniel J. Townsend, wit. Mar Set 8: 140-144

Townsend, Thomas & Miss Mary Magdalen Miller, 12 Dec 1810, in St. Philip's Church. St Phil PR

Trapier, Benjamin Foissin & Hannah Shubrick Heyward, 23 Dec 1802; Mary Irvine, Susannah Keith, J. H. Stevens, wit. Mar Set 4: 278-281

Trapier, Benjamin Foissin of Charleston and wife Hannah Shubrick Trapier, formerly Hannah Shubrick Heyward, 16 July 1806; Thomas Shubrick, Nathaniel Heyward, William Heyward, trustees; Ben. F. Trapier, wit. Mar Set 5: 218-220

Trapier, Paul & Sarah Alicia Shubrick, daughter of Thomas Shubrick, 6 Jan 1802; M. Irvine, Jno Keith, wit. Mar Set 4: 168

Trapier, Paul Esq. of Georgetown, & Miss Sarah Shubrick, of Charleston, 7 Jan 1802. St Phil PR

Trapman, John Louis & Mary Bowen Moore of Charleston, daughter of John Elias Moore, decd., 13 Nov 1819; Robert Hume, trustee; W. S. Campbell, Daniel Jennings Waring, wit. Mar Set 8: 66-72

Trescott, John and Miss Caroline Carriere, 19 March 1816 in Charleston. St Phil PR

Trescott, Joseph & Miss Caroline Flagg, 12 Feb 1815, in Charleston. St Phil PR

Trescott, William & Caroline Markley, 29 Dec 1814, in Charleston. St Phil PR

Trezevant, John F. of Charleston, attorney at law, & Margaret P. Gignilliat of McIntosh County, Ga., 12 May 1813; James Nephew, of "same county & state" (McIntosh County, Ga.?), & Edward W. North of Coosawhatchie, S. C.,trustees; Rob Bentham, John Gignilliat, wit. Mar Set 6: 296-299

Truchelut, Jean Baptist & Louise Dufours, 8 Oct 1814. St Mary's RC

Truchelut, Joseph, merchant, resident in Charleston, native of Rekon, Department de la Moselle, son of Joseph Truchelut and wife Marie Jeanne Gite, and Caroline Marie Saute, 20 Sept 1809 (original in French). Mar Set 6: 91-96

Tucker, Benjamin of Georgetown, & Sarah Heriot Tucker of same, 15 Nov 1804; John Tucker, trustee; Geo Heriot, C DuPre, wit. Mar Set 4: 461-466

Tucker, John H. & Elizabeth Ann Allston, daughter of Benjamin Allston Junior, of All Saints Parish, 12 Jan 1809; A. Marvin, wit. Mar Set 5: 438-440

Tunis, Charles Humphries, of Charleston, factor, & Margaret Ann Mitchell, of Charleston, spinster, 19 March 1814; license to Dr. John Buchan. Chaston Pro J

Tunno, Thomas & Harriet Ward, 26 April 1800; Thomas Mathews & Joshua Ward the younger, trustees; John Ward, John Price, wit. Mar Set 3: 450-453

Turnbull, Joseph & Nancy Mecklin, 26 Feb 1807. Moses Waddel

Turnbull, William, late from India but now at Charleston, & Eliza Catherine Percy, third daughter of the Rev. William Percy, 16 Feb 1805; Thomas Bainbridge of Upper-Guilford Street, Russell Square, London, trustee; Bard. Elliott, Richard B. Baker, wit. Mar Set 5: 495-496

Turner, John & Elizabeth Mooney, 15 Sept 1818 in Charleston. St Phil PR

Ulmer, David & Elenar McWhirter, 7 Nov 1805. Bryan Journal

Ulmer, Paul of village of Coosawhatchie, & Maria Wilson, of Combahee, spinster, 22 Dec 1819; James Sharpe, Samuel N. Hamelton, both of Colleton Dist., trustees; A. W. Davis, William Royall Junr., wit. Mar Set 8: 95-96

Ulmot, Antoine Europe, surgeon, native of Colonier, province of Languedoc, & Marie Louise Aimee Champy, born Isle Guadaloupe, daughter of Mr. Edrne Champy and wife Marie Barbe Arsouneau Beausejou, 19 Aug 1800; bride has resided in Charleston with her parents 6 years. (original in French, translated BHH). Mar Set 3: 475-476

Vandermissin, Chevalier Louisa Jaques Dominique & wife Louisa Catherine Colleton Vandermissin, daughter of Richard Graves and wife Louisa Carolina, 21 July 1817; John Secker Jr., John Clode, wit. Mar Set 7: 265-269

Vaughan, Thomas of Kershaw Dist., & Mary Harmon, daughter of Stephen Harmon of same, 28 Feb 1816; John Robertson, trustee; James F. Seale, Burrel Harmon, wit. Misc Rec C, pp. 291-292

Vaux, Percival Edward of Waccamaw, All Saints Parish, and Sarah Richards, 19 Dec 1805; Daniel Hall, trustee; Robert D. Lawrence, wit. Mar Set 5: 130-131

Veigneau, John of St. Luke's Parish, farmer & Sarah Worster, of St. Peter's Parish, 12 Aug 1818; David Hennis, Sampson Worster, trustee; Thos. A. Thompson, Richd. Y. Carey, wit. Mar Set 7: 293-295

Veitch, Henry, of St. Paul, planter, & Margaret Morrison, of St. Bartholomew, spinster, 13 May 1808, to Rev. Thomas Mills. Chaston ML

Verdier, Alexander H. & Elinor Fleming, 23 Sept 1809. St Hel PR

Vernon, Nathaniel & Eliza Ann Russell, 18 Aug 1814, in Charleston. St Phil PR

Vernon, Richard & Rebekah Ward, 14 Jan 1808. Moses Waddel

Vernon, Robert & Eliza Ward, 27 Feb 1806. Moses Waddel

Verree, George of Charleston, Esqr., & Rebecca Jerman of St James Parish, spinster, 19 Jan 1803; Thomas Satur Jerman, Joseph Verree, trustee; E. W. Weyman, Saml Verree, John Teasdale Jr., wit. Mar Set 4: 274-278

Verree, John & Miss Elizabeth Theus, free persons of color, 18 March 1818 in Charleston. St Phil PR

Versen, William Sr. of Georgetown, & Eliza Wilkes of the same, 15 Oct 1800; Cornelius Dupre, trustee; Eleanor Davis, Abram Myers, wit. Mar Set 3: 479-482

Vesey, Joseph W. & Miss Sarah Duprat, free persons of color, 17 Dec 1818 in Charleston. St Phil PR

Vigie, Antoine & Julie Belmont, widow, Boulanger, 14 Aug 1804; E. Pohl, Fleury Louis, wit. Mar Set 5: 186-187

Vincent, Louis & Margarite Betard, 24 Jan 1813. St Mary's RC

Vincent, Thomas of Charleston & Elizabeth Murphey, 4 May 1801; George Macauley, trustee; James S. Neilson, Jas. Nicholson, wit. Mar Set 4: 73-77

Vonhagen, George of Charleston, grocer, to Sarah Smith, of Charleston, widow, to Rev. Charles Faber, 19 Jan 1811. Chaston ML

Wagner, Effingham of Charleston, merchant & Franciade M. Godard, of Charleston, spinster, 6 Nov 1815; license to Rt. Rev. Dr. Theo. Dehon. Chaston Pro J

Wagner, George of Charleston, merchant, & Charlotte Ogier Martin, of Charleston, spinster, 24 Sept 1816; license to Right Revd. Dr. Theodore Dehon. Chaston Pro J

Wagner, Jasper & Margaret Wood, of Charleston, widow, 23 Dec 1811; Robert Stent, trustee; William Wadsworth, Joseph L. Enlow, wit. Mar Set 6: 110-112

Walker, Daniel & Margaret Curry, 24 Dec 1807. Bryan Journal

Walker, John W. & Matilda Pope, 30 Jan 1810. Moses Waddel

Walker, Langford, & Polly Harper, 25 June 1812. Moses Waddel

Walker, Posy & Mary Magouley, 26 Dec 1819. Bryan Journal

Walker, Richard & Miss Eliza Boyden, 25 Aug 1816 in Charleston. St Phil PR

Walker, Steven & Maryan Strickland, 25 Nov 1802. Bryan Journal

Waller, William & Maria Thomson Mayberry, 22 Oct 1812 in Charleston. St Phil PR

Walling, Elisha & wife Elizabeth, __ May 1808; Daniel Walling, Samuel Huff, trustees; Peter Blewer, Catharine Blewer, wit. Mar Set 5: 456-458

Walsh, John & Miss Eliza A. Mackenzie (colored persons), 7 Feb 1816 in Charleston. St Phil PR

Walsh, Robert F. & Dorothy Michau, both of Williamsburg District, 21 Aug 1815; Caleb C. Lenud, Alexander Michau, trustee; Jon. Perdriau, Charlotte Lenud, Ann Perdriau, wit. Mar Set 6: 413-417

Walsh, Robert F. & Dorothy Michau, 21 Aug 1815; Caleb C. Lenud, Alexander Michau, trustees; Jon. Perdriau, Charlotte Lenud, Ann Perdriau, wit. Wmbg DB B, pp. 164-166

Walten, Christopher B. & Eliza Johnson, both of Charleston, 31 Dec 1813; James Robinson, Jno Phillips White, wit. Mar Set 6: 294-296

Walton, Newel & _____ Walton, __ April 1800. Moses Waddel

Walton, William of Charleston, & Justina Louisa Gennerick,
daughter of John Frederick Gennerick, 3 Feb 1807;
Willm Turpin, Whiteford Smith, wit. Mar Set 5: 274-
283

Ward, Walter & Elizabeth Smith, 26 April 1810. Moses
Waddel

Ware, Robert & Eliza Stanton, 20 Dec 1805. Moses Waddel

Waring, Joseph H. & Miss Martha Waring, 11 June 1811, in
St. George's Parish. St Phil PR

Waring, Thomas the younger of Pine hill in St. George's
Parish, planter, & Mrs. Sarah Ladson of St. Paul's
Parish, widow, 1 Jan 1800; James Boone, John Mitchell,
and William Boone Mitchell, Esqrs., trustees; Morton
Waring, Edith Waring, Ann Waring, wit. Mar Set 3, pp.
416-418

Warley, Jacob & Miss Sophia Fraser, 18 Dec 1815, in St.
Bartholomew's Parish. St Phil PR

Warley, William-Kern of Charleston, physician, & Mary-
Motte Wilson, of Charleston, spinster, to Rev. James
D. Simons, 13 April 1810. Chaston ML

Warnock, John & Herriott Cape, married 9 Oct 1814; Israel
Munds, trustee; marriage settlement dated 31 March
1815; Isaac Griggs, John Saml Courtney, wit. Mar Set
6: 381-383

Warnock, Thomas of Charleston, gentleman, & Mary Boyden,
widow, 15 April 1813; Jacob Henry, storekeeper, trustee; Alfred Augustus Lonely, wit. Mar Set 6: 254-255

Warren, John A. & Miss Anna O. Pritchard, 25 Nov 1819 in
Charleston. St Phil PR

Wartenberg, Peter of Charleston, grocer, & Mary-Catharine
Boyer, of Charleston, spinster, to Rev. Charles Faber,
4 May 1810. Chaston ML

Watkins, Robert H. & Prudence Oliver, 25 April 1805.
Moses Waddel

Watkins, William & Ruth Pope, 15 May 1806. Moses Waddel

Watkinson, John & Frances White of Charleston, widow, 4
May 1813; Christopher Nelson, trustee; Isaac Griggs,
Richd Wall, wit. Mar Set 6: 208-209

Way, Matthew, son of William & Abbigal Way, Marlborough
Dist., S.C., & Agness Moorman, daughter of Thomas &
Susannah Moorman, Richmond Co.,N.C.,1 Jan 1806. Piney
Grove MM

Way, Paul, son of William & Abigal Way, Marlborough Dist.,
S. C., & Achsah Moorman, daughter of John & Rebeckah
Moorman, Richmond Co., N. C., 22 Oct 1806. Piney
Grove MM

Wayne, Jacob & Elizabeth Lesesne of Georgetown, 15 June
1811; John Wragg, Joseph Lesesne, trustees; Saml
Smith Jr., Peter Cooper, wit. Mar Set 6: 79-81

Webb, Daniel Canno of Charleston, factor, & Elizabeth
Ladson (daughter of Thomas Ladson, late of Island of
St. Helena, Beaufort District), 28 Nov 1805; Benjamin
Jenkins & Benjamin Chaplin, surviving executors of the
last will & testament of sd. Thomas Ladson; Thomas
Foster, trustee; Charles G. Capers, Glen Drayton, wit.
Mar Set 5: 101-111

Webb, William, merchant, & Caroline I'ans Thorne, spinster,
22 April 1817; John Gardner Thorne, trustee; Nathaniel
Slawson, Jno S. Thorne, wit. Mar Set 7: 186-189

Weed, John & Anne Spence, 26 Aug 1813. Moses Waddel

Weed, Joseph B. and Miss Susan Wade, 9 April 1817 in
Charleston. St Phil PR

Welch, James & Mary Sutherland, 15 Aug 1816. Moses
Waddel

Welch, John of Parish of St. Bartholomew & Mary Ann
Hamilton, 25 June 1801; Thos. D. Bladen, John Hood,
wit. Mar Set 4: 91-92

Welch, Nathaniel of village of Islington, S. C., & Elizabeth Heft, spinster, 10 April 1813; Thomas Welch of
Charleston, trustee; Othniel J. Giles, Rachel Sheppard,
wit. Mar Set 6: 237-239

Welsh, Samuel of Charleston, & Mrs. Elizabeth Gordon,
widow, 24 Feb 1802; Keating Simons, trustee; Edward
Simons, wit. Mar Set 4: 145-146

Wells, Robert & Catharine Heckell, 26 Feb 1804. St
Matthews Luth Ch

Wells, Robert & Martha Garden, colored persons, 12 Oct
1815 in Charleston. St Phil PR

Whetstone, Jacob & Mary Hanson, 4 Aug 1803. St Matthews
Luth Ch

Whilden, Joseph & Mary Magdalene Sire, 28 May 1814. St
Mary's RC

Whitaker, Lam. & Eliz. Brown, 28 Jan 1800. Kershaw Diary

White, George King & Rebecca Chambers, 14 Nov 1804; Thomas Rivers Junr, Joshua Player, Aaron Thompson, trustees; James Fogartie, John S. Rose, wit. Mar Set 4:
503-508

White, James & Sarah Stevens, 8 Oct 1801. Bryan Journal

White, James of Georgetown Dist., & Mary Eliza Palmer, of
same, 3 Jan 1820; Jesse Palmer, Loammi Palmer, trustees;
Catherine Palmer, Burral Burd, wit. Mar Set 8: 76-78

White, James Jeremiah Brickell, of Chaleston, & Mary
Elizabeth Dupre, of St. James Santee Parish, spinster,
15 May 1817; Samuel Warren, planter, trustee; L. A.
Perdreau, William A. Brickell, John Blake White, wit.
Mar Set 7: 192-195

White, John Captn of Scr Little Emily & Jane Keyes, 8
Nov 1819 at Winyaw Bay. Pro Geo Winyaw

White, John B. & Miss Anna Rachel O'Driscoll, 1 Oct 1819
in Charleston. St Phil PR

White, John Blake of Charleston & Eliza Allston, spinster,
of Georgetown, _____ 1805; William Allston of Georgetown, physician, and James Brickell of St. John's
Parish, also physician, trustees; John Cogdell, Wm.
Trandolph Theus, wit. Mar Set 5: 29-35

White, Stephen & Rebeckah Stuart, 23 Dec 1806. Bryan
Journal

White, Thomas Penny of Weymouth Street, Parish of St.
Mary le Bone, Clerk Fellow of Queen's College Cambridge,
& Charlotte Eliza Channing, late of Staines in Middlesex County, now of Beaumont Street, Parish of St. Mary
le Bone, spinster, 2 Dec 1812; John Calcutta White of
Pembroke Hall, University of Cambridge, James Duppa
of Oxford Street, Co. of Middlesex, paper hanger, trustee; Chas. May, Francis Fladgate, wit. Mar Set 7: 12-
28

Whitefield, George & Rebekah Freeman, 22 Jan 1807. Moses
Waddel

Whitefield, Joseph T. & Martha Griffin, 9 Dec 1819. Moses
Waddel

Wickham, Thomas T. of Catfish & Ann Shackelford of Brittons Neck, 15 Oct 1800; license directed to Revd.
Thomas Humphries. Marion ML

Wideman, Henry & _____ Roberts, 30 April 1818. Moses
Waddel

Wigfall, Levi Durand of Christ Church Parish, & Eliza
    Thomson, of Charleston, spinster, 3 Nov 1802; Lewis
    Trezebant, William Johnson, and Thomas Hall, trustees;
    Joshua Player, wit. Mar Set 4: 209-219

Wigfall, Thomas of St. Thomas's Parish, Esqr., & Eliza
    Moore Flagg, spinster, 13 Dec 1813; George Flagg, Hugh
    Patterson, trustees; Maurice Simons Jr., Ebenezer Flagg,
    wit. Mar Set 6: 291-293

Wigfall, Thomas & Eliza Flagg, 15 Dec 1813, in Charleston.
    St Phil PR

Wightman, John T. & Miss Eliza Stoll, 2 Dec 1818 in
    Charleston. St Phil PR

Wilcocks, Samuel of Philadelphia, counsellor at law &
    Harriet Manigault of same, daughter of Gabriel Mani-
    gault of Charleston, decd., 29 May 1816; Charles Jared
    Ingersoll, Charles Izard Manigault, trustees; Saml.
    Wilcocks, Jos. Reed, wit. Mar Set 7: 238-240

Wilcox, Samuel W. & Mary Ann Louisa McCan, daughter of
    Edward McCan, decd., 18 June 1818; Samuel McGinley and
    wife Jerusha, late Jerusha McCan, widow of Edward Mc-
    Can, and mother of Mary Ann L., trustees; Dr. James
    E. B. Finley, trustee; Robt. F. Burdell, John Dougherty,
    wit. Mar Set 7: 277-282

Wilkes, John, late of New York, now of Charleston, &
    Clelia Lightwood, daughter of Elizabeth Lightwood, 3
    Nov 1819; E. Lightwood, Wm. Peronneau, wit. Mar Set
    8: 65-66

Wilkie, James Esq., of Charleston, & Sarah Mazyck, of
    Charleston, spinster, 5 Dec 1816; license to the Revd.
    Doctor William Percy. Chaston Pro J

Wilkie, William B. & Caroline Teasdale, 13 Jan 1816, in
    Charleston. St Phil PR

Wilkins, Gov. Morris of New York City, gentleman, and
    Mary Somersall Ward, eldest daughter of John Ward,
    late of Charleston, decd., 20 Apr 1819; Fs. Motte, Z.
    Bradish, wit. Mar Set 8: 54-57

Wilkinson, William of St. Bartholomew's Parish, & Amarin-
    thia Jenkins of Edisto Island, spinster, 23 March 1813;
    Benjamin Seabrook of Edisto Island, trustee; Daniel
    Townsend, John Mikell Senr, wit. Mar Set 6: 201-205

Wilkinson, Willis of Georgetown, physician, & Eleanor
    Withers, 11 Dec 1806; Robert F. Withers, trustee; Susan
    Hails, Jno Shackelford, wit. Mar Set 5: 286-291

Willet, Jno. S. & Miss Eliza Richardson, 5 May 1814.
Kershaw Diary

William, slave of Miss Fayssoux, & Nelly, slave of Mrs.
Arch Brown, 18 March 1813, in Charleston. St Phil PR

William, slave of Christopher Fitzsimons, and Kitty, slave
of David Deas, 5 Jan 1816, in Charleston. St Phil PR

William, slave of Mr. John Johnson, & Sarah, slave of Mrs.
Meers, Oct 1816 in Charleston. St Phil PR

William, slave of Thomas Corbett Senr & Harriet, slave of
Dr. Alexr Baron Senr, 16 June 1813, in Charleston. St
Phil PR

William & Clara, slaves of P. Gadsden family, 30 Dec 1814,
in Charleston. St Phil PR

William, slave of Dr. Reed & Dorcas, slave of Mr. Jno
Holmes, of St. Michael's Church, rector being sick, 1
Aug 1817 in Mazyckborough. St Phil PR

Williman, Christopher of Charleston, Esquire, & Sarah
Simpson Baron, of Charleston, spinster, 11 Dec 1815;
license to Rt. Revd. Theo. Dehon or Revd. Andrew
Forster. Chaston Pro J

Willington, Aaron S., & Ann L. Course, 21 April 1814, in
Georgetown, S. C. St Phil PR

Willis, John Hancock, of Charleston, merchant, & Mary-
Hannah Gabeau, of Charleston, spinster, 29 Aug 1808.
Chaston ML

Wilmer, Jonathan R., of Maryland, attorney, & Sarah
Reeves Gibbes, 26 Jan 1801; Lewis Gibbes, trustee;
Alexr. Garden, wit. Mar Set 4: 9-11

Wilson, Alexr. Baron of Charleston, Esquire, & Sophia
Frances Perry Shepheard, of Charleston, spinster, 15
Nov 1816; license to the Revd. Dr. William Percy.
Chaston Pro J

Wilson, Alexander Barron & Sophia F. Shepheard, minor
daughter of Mrs. Sophia F. Shepheard, 16 Nov 1816;
William Hasell Gibbes, William Trescot, trustees;
Amelia H. McCall, Ann D. McCall, Elizabeth Hamilton
McCall, wit. Mar Set 7: 90-96

Wilson, Christopher, son of John & Dinah Wilson, Union
Dist., & Mary Cox, daughter of Thomas & Tamar Cox,
Union Dist., 25 Dec 1800. Cane Cr MM

Wilson, Hamilton & Mary Howard, _____ 1801. Moses Waddel

Wilson, James & Margaret Watson, 26 March 1819. Moses Waddel

Wilson, John of Georgetown Dist., & Ann Dollard of same, widow, 6 May 1801; Daniel O Hara, Thomas Chapman, William Falconer, Esqrs., trustees; Wm. Know, P. Donnelly, Jno Martin, wit. Mar Set 4: 56-62

Wilson, John & Polly Shoemaker, 20 March 1811. Moses Waddel

Wilson, John & Miss Eliza Gibbs, 22 Jan 1811, in St. Michael's Parish. St Phil PR

Wilson, John & Frances Ann Freer, 27 April 1814 in Charleston. St Phil PR

Wilson, Robert & Charity Latham, spinster, 20 Nov 1800. St Phil PR

Wilson, Robert K. and Nancy Beaty, 28 May 1801, consent by Elizabeth Beaty, mother, signed at Yorkville. York Pro 66/3117

Wilson, Samuel Dr. & Miss Mary Mazyck, 14 May 1816 in Charleston. St Phil PR

Wilson, William, a free colored man & Jenny, slave of Mr. Vernon, 4 June 1817 in Charleston. St Phil PR

Wilson, William S. & Charlotte Whitfield, 11 Dec 1806. Moses Waddel

Windham, Daniel & Martha Benton, 13 March 1819. Bryan Journal

Wingard, Samuel & Catharine Bickley, 22 Jan 1808. St Michaels Luth Ch

Wingard, William & Elender Burge, 26 Oct 1819. Drehr Journal

Winthrop, Joseph A. of Charleston, & Mary Eveline Parker, daughter of Thomas Parker, 18 Feb 1818; Edwin Parker, Charles Parker, wit. Mar Set 7: 233-236

Wise, Frederick & Julia Kelley, 30 June 1814. St Michaels Luth Ch

Wise, George & Molly Roberts, 5 Oct 1819. Drehr Journal

Wise, Emanuel & Mary Heffernon, 2 May 1819. St Mary's RC

Wissenhunt, George & Catherine Miegler, 21 May 1811. St
Matthews Luth Ch

Withers, Robert of Waccamaw & Miss Mary Eleonora Mayrant,
4 April 1820. Holy Cross Ch

Witherspoon, Robert B. & Sarah Lane, widow, both of Williamsburgh Dist., 24 Sept 1818; Stephen Miller the
elder, Thomas Witherspoon, trustees; Thos Steel, John
T. Williams, John W. Swinton, wit. Mar Set 7: 304-309

Witherspoon, Robert B. & Sarah Lane, 24 Sept 1818; Stephen
Miller the elder, Thomas Witherspoon, trustees; Tho.
Steel, John T. Williams, John W. Swinton, wit. Wmbg
DB B, pp. 239-241

Wittencamp, Charles & Ann Jones, 23 Jan 1814, in Charleston. St Phil PR

Woodberry, Richard Jr. of Brittons Neck, & Desdemona Davis
of same, both of Marion Dist., 17 Jan 1801; license
directed to William Palmer. Marion ML

Woodruff, Major James Joseph and Miss Jane Harris, 8
Feb 1816 in Charleston. St Phil PR

Woodrupp, John of Charleston, merchant, & Ann McCall, of
the same place, spinster, 1 Oct 1800. St Phil PR

Woodward, Elisha & Esther Lepear of Georgetown, 12 Feb
1807; Samuel Smith, Isaac Course, trustees; William
Grant, Samuel Smith Jr., wit. Mar Set 5: 336-339

Woolcock, William, of Charleston, house carpenter, and
Ann Taylor, of the same place, widow, 2 March 1802.
St Phil PR

Woolsey, Abram M. & Emily W. Sims, 26 Jan 1820. Moses
Waddel

Wooten, Abram & Fanny Ford al. Vickry, 6 Aug 1812. Moses
Waddel

Wotten, Christopher B. & Eliza Johnson, 1 Jan 1814. 2d
Pres Ch

Wotton, John & Elisabeth Dash, 24 Nov 1811. St Matthews
Luth Ch

Wragg, Samuel of Charleston, & Mary Ashby I'on, daughter
of Jacob Bond I'on, decd., 19 Feb 1801; Jacob Bon I'on,
Thomas Lowndes, trustees; Miss Jane Graham, wit. Mar
Set 4: 14-21

Wragg, Samuel and Mary Ashby I'on, spinster, 19 Feb 1801.
St Phil PR

Wright, Charles C. and Miss Lavinia Simons, 18 Sept 1820
in Charleston. St Phil PR

Wright, Joseph, & Mary Twitty, to Rev. Joshua Lewis, 6
Dec 1807. Marlboro ML

Wright, Thomas of Charleston, & Eliza McCormick, widow,
19 Sept 1811; John Everingtham of Charleston, Thomas
Mackie of Philadelphia, trustees; Wm Marshall, Wm. M.
Scott, Geo. R. Logan, wit. Mar Set 6: 63-67

Wright, William, son of Nathan Wright, & Mary Mill(s),
daughter of John Mills, Newberry Dist., S. C., 30 Nov
1800. Bush R MM

Wright, William of St. Bartholomew's Parish, & Elizabeth
Cannon, widow, 5 April 1817; Samson W. Letih, M. D.
& William Patterson Jr., planter, trustees; Henry
Cannon, Nathaniel Langley, wit. Mar Set 7: 175-177

Wyatt, John A. & Miss Eliza Moon, 28 March 1816, in
Charleston. St Phil PR

Wyld, John C. of Colleton Dist., & Margaret Stone of same,
6 Dec 1804; Gilbert Chalmers, trustee; Sophia Chalmers,
John Geddes, wit. Mar Set 4: 466-471

Young, Thomas of Waccamaw, Parish of All Saints, & Mary,
daughter of William Allston the younger decd., 24 April
1800; Henry Collins Flagg, John Moore, of the Parish of
St. Thos & St. Dennis, trustees; Jno Magill, Eliza
Gibbes, Mary Young, wit. Mar Set 3: 453-462

Ziegler, George & Rachell Fogel, _____ 1807. St Matthews
Luth Ch

Ziegler, Jacob & Margeret Sellers, 5 June 1810. St
Matthews Luth Ch

Ziegler, John & Rosina Speignerd, 17 Aug 1806. St. Matthews Luth Ch

INDEX

Bessilleau, Johanna 97
Best, William (Dr.) 85
Betard, Margarite 119
Beverly, Mary 10
Beze, Joanna 93
Bibb, Dolly 95
  Martha 41
Bickley, Catharine 126
Bickly, Caroline 26
  Lucy 87
Bigelow, Martha 78
Bigger, Mary Ann 87
  Moses 87
Billing, Eliza (Mrs.) 29
Bineham, Benjamin 46
Bishop, Charles (Capt.) 15
  Jane 15
  John 85
Bizeul, Marie Bodine
    Modeste 71
Black, Charles 11, 74
  Jean 87
  John 60
  Sarah Hanson 11
Blackley, Louisa 4
Blacklock, Katherine 37
  William 37
Blackmon, Thos. 57
Blackwell, Elizabeth 49
Bladen, Thos. D. 66, 122
Blair, James 47
  Joseph 100
Blake, Jane S. 2
Blamyer, Caroline 109
  William 109
Blandin, Catherine 90
Blewer, Catharine 120
  Catherine 42
  Peter 120
Blocker, Abner 11
  Eliza. 10, 11
  James 97
  John, Jr. 11
  Mary 31
  Sarah 9
Blyth, Elizabeth F. 22
Blythe, Joseph 106
Boggs, Elizabeth 110
  Martha 110
Boid, Margaret 40
Boillat, Elizabeth 47
Boirot, Catherine 102
Bolan, Richard 113
Bolles, John T. 105

Bond, Henry 35
  Sarah 27
Bone, Mary le 123
Bonhost, William Joseph 80
Bonneau, (?) (Mrs.) 97
  Elizabeth 27
  Francis 27
  Sabina 107
  Sarah Eleanor 27
Bonnell, Rebecca 103
Bookter, Jacob 7
  Judith 7
Boone, James 68, 121
  Maria 41
  Mary S. 41
  Susan 31
  Thomas 31, 41
  Thos 85
Booner, Ann (Mrs.) 26
Boozer, (?) 105
Bouchanneau, Elizabeth 81
Boucheneau, Mary Ann 16
Boucher, Mary 35
Bouchillon, Susan 84
Boulanger, (?) (Widow) 119
Boulger, John (Rev.) 24
Bounetheau, Elizabeth-Bond
  97
Bourquin, Susan G. 41, 74
Boutillier, Marie Francoise
  113
Bow, Ann (Mrs.) 22
Bowen, Nathaniel (Rev.) 56
  Nathl. (Rev.) 42
Bowering, Martha 55
Bowie, James 41
Bowler, James Henry 38
  Sarah E. 60
Bowman, (?) 29
  Eliza Allston 42
  James 72, 105
  Mary 74
  Sarah 102
Bowmans, (?) 103
Boyd, H. A. 15
  Wm 50
Boyden, Eliza 120
  Mary 121
Boyer, Mary-Catharine 121
Boykin, Kitty 70
Boylston, N. H. 13, 18, 64
Boyter, Danl 20
Bracey, A. J. 81
  X. J. 81

134

Bracy, Marriah 80
Bradford, Sarah 26
Bradish, Z. 124
Bradley, Nancy 27
Brady, Jane 85
Brailsford, Anna Maria 43
 Mary 56
Brandeburg, Magdelen 43
 Margaret 43
 Mary 105
Brandt, Hannah 13
Branes, Sarah 13
Branford, B. 106
 Sarah 91
 Sarah T. 15
Brantly, W. T. 95
Braund, Mary 76
Breazeal, Nancy 77
 Barbara 102
Brebner, Archibald 36
Breed, Lucy 1
Bressat, Alexandre 14
Brevard, Martha 31
Brickell, James 123
 William A. 123
Bride, Elizabeth 67
Bright, Elizabeth 32
 Frances 91
 Mary 1
Brightman, Ann Moore 18
Brimner, Dianah Young 26
Brisbane, (?) 3
 John 46
 Maria 32
 Sarah H. 46
Broadrick, Mary Madeline 37
Brock, Eleanor 104
 Jane 10
 Margaret 80
Brockington, Penelope 10
Broderick, Mary 37
Brodie, (?) (Mrs.) 94
 Robt, Jr. 26
Brogdon, Moses 20
Broughton, Alexander 15
 Charlotte 51
 Daniel 15
 Elizabeth Damaris 15
 James 15
 Mary 15
Brower, Christiana 25
Brown, Ann Eliza 83
 Arch (Mrs.) 125
 Duncan (Rev.) 7, 36

Brown (cont.)
 E. G. 34
 Effie 93
 Eleanor 109
 Eliz. 122
 Eliza Ann 89
 Elsey 17
 F. B. T. 5
 James 46, 108
 Jane 4
 Joshua 70
 Mary 16
 Mary Ann Rebekah 74
 Rebecca (Mrs.) 18
 Rose 72
 Samuel 46
 Sarah 7
 Sims 41
 Wilson 69
Browne, A. J. 49
 Robert 99
Brownfield, Rd. 3
 Robert 55
Bruce, Susanna 9, 110
 Derdrick Julius 23
 Mary 23
Brunson, Jonathan 16
Bryan, Delilah 26
 Fortunatus 74
 Jon 9
 Joseph 97, 105
 Matilda S. 28
 Mehetabel 53
Buchan, John (Dr.) 118
 John (Rev.) 4, 19, 20,
  112
Buchanan, Elizabeth 8
Buche, Margaret 92
Buckeley, Elizabeth 56
Buckle, Mary 60
Buckmyer, John C. 82
Bugg, Charlotte 89
Buist, George (Rev.) 3, 43
Bull, William Robert 111
 Wm. S. 97
Bullard, Julah 1
Buntin, Owen 97
Burbridge, Arthur 17
 Thomas 17
Burch, Mary (Mrs.) 67
 Mary A. 113
Burckmyer, J. 101
Burd, Burral 123
Burdell, Robert 64

Burdell (cont.)
  Robt. F. 124
Burden, Mary 17
  Thomas 17
Burge, Elender 126
Burger, Saml 30
Burges, James 63
  Mary Margaret 63
Burgess, Edward 16
  James 34, 104
Buris, Jane M. 48
Burkett, Elisabeth 86
  Sophia 13
Burnet, Mary D. 39
Burnett, Joseph 9
Burwell, Cradk. 4
Bush, Providence 64
Butcher, Mary 18
Buyck, A. 86
Byers, Elizabeth 94
  William 94
Byrd, John J. 113
Byrnes, Elizabeth 89
Cades, Elizabeth 52
  James 52
  Thomas 52
Cadet, Gomez 66
Caije, Marie Eulalie 31
Cain, Eliza 89
Calahan, Mary 106
Calden, James 110
Caldwell, Eliza 111
  Jane 65
  John 108
Calhoun, Catharine 12
  Jane 68, 113
  Maria 50
Callum, Susannah 92
Cambridge, Ann 19
  J. H. 101
  Tobias 19, 91
Cameron, Mary-Elizabeth 18
Campbell, (?) (Mrs.) 115
  Alexander 112
  Ann (Mrs.) 105
  Edward W. 105
  James M. 41
  John 7
  John B. 24
  Margaret E. 47
  Maria An (Mrs.) 19
  W. S. 117
  Wm. 101
Cannon, Elizabeth 128

Cannon (cont.)
  Henry 128
  Martha 115
  Mary 112
Canter, Charlotte 104
  Jacob 104
  Joshua 104
Cantey, Elizabeth Bland-
    ford 52
  James 52
  Margaret 109
Canty, Saml 75
Capdeville, Mary (Mrs.)
    100
Cape, Herriott 121
  Providence G. A. (Mrs.)
    96
  Providence G. Adams (Mrs.)
    96
Capers, (?) (Rev.) 12
  Charles G. 122
  Eliza 108
  Mary 20
  William 6, 52, 102
  William (Rev.) 83, 85
Cardind, John E. 47
Carendeffox, Louise
    Charlotte Amelie 81
Carey, Richd. Y. 119
Carlton, Ann 32
Carmichael, Catherine 20
Carne, Thomas Wm 86
Carr, Ann 98
  Isaac 44
  Judith 21
  Mary 73
  Thomas 23, 109
Carrel, Joseph, Sr. 21
Carriere, Caroline 117
Carrol, Eliza 99
  Joanna 99
Carroll, Honora 52
  Mary 52
  Mary Ann 67
  Rachel G. 92
Carrth, John 34
Carson, Elizabeth 14
  Laura Elizabeth 14
  William 60
Carter, Mary 28
Cartwright, Paul A. 36
Carvalko, E. N. 61
Cary, Henry 14
Casolot, Elizabeth 38

Cassels, John 3
Castel, Mariam 98
Chalbo, Maryan 62
Chalmers, David 54
  Gilbert 128
  Sophia 128
Chambers, Rebecca 101, 123
Champion, Richard Lloyd
  46
Champy, Edrne 118
  Marie Louise 118
Chancognie, Louis
    Charles Francois 22
  Montel 22
Chanler, Eliza 89
  Elizabeth 83
Channing, Charlotte Eliza
  123
Chanson, H. 86
Chaplain, Archibald 100
  Mary E. 100
Chaplin, Benjamin 122
  Edwin 100
  Eliza 100
  John L. 74
Chapman, (?) 114
  Thomas 19, 79, 126
  W. 106
Charles, Edgar W. 88
Chartier, Jean Jacques
  113
Chaten, Ann 72
Cheramy, Frans. 34
Cherry, Mary 56
Cherrytree, Anne 58
Chesnut, Marg. 29
  Mary 30
Chevard, Vincent 23
Cheves, Langdon 54, 77
  Susanna 77
Chevillette, Louisa 101
Chiffelle, Ann A. 108
  Ann Alicia 112
  Thomas P. 112
Chinners, Sarah Ann
    Elizabeth 23
Chisolm, Sarah Maxwell
  44
Chitty, J. W. 57
Chivers, Ann 44
Choinard, Charles 88
Chovin, Elizabeth 17
Christian, Mary L. 105
Christie, Alexr 47

Clark, Eliza 24
  Elizabeth 19
  Jane 38, 89
  John 24
  Margaret 24
  Mary 53, 82
  Robert 110
  Susan 14
  William 82
  Wm. 8
Clarke, John 4
  Mary 73
Clarkson, Alexander 100
  Eliza 40
  Mary Magdaline 100
  William 15, 22
  William, Jr. 22
Claudonsen, Felicite 101
Cleapor, Ann Louisa 21
  Maria E. 33
Cleary, Eliza Ann 32
  Nathaniel G. 31
Clement, Eleanor 64
  John M. 86
  William 86
  Wm. 60
Clifton, C. 21
Clitheral, Mary 69
Clitherall, George 27, 115
  Mary Magdalene Inglis
    115
Close, John 118
Coachman, Mary 2
  Mary Adeline 24
Coat, Marmaduke 24
Coate, Marmaduke 24
Cobb, Martha J. 62
Cochran, Lotitia 24
Cogdell, John 54, 123
  John S. 33, 47, 53, 62,
    114
  Richard W. 13
Coggeshall, Nathl 110
Cohen, Bella 25
  Celia 25
  Dinah 83
  Hannah 25
  Jacob 55, 93
  Jacob J. 86
  Jane 85
  Lewin 110
  Myer 86
  P. 86
  Robert 4

137

Drayton (cont.)
  Glen 88, 122
  Maria-Henrietta 45
Drehr, Ann 33, 107
  John 33
Dubart, Mary 88
Dubbert, Frederick 37
Duboe, Francois 116
Dubois, Louis 22
  Louisa 22, 23
Dubose, Elizabeth 34
  Harriet 67
  Jos. 29
  Mary R. 4
  Saml 29
  Samuel 109, 110
Dubuard, Peter Francis
  100
Dudley, Mary 56
Due, Francis 102
Duffey, Abigil 65
  Henry 5
Dufours, Louise 117
Duke, Harriet 25
  John 7
Dulles, Joseph 45
Dumont, Ursule 104
Duncan, James 47
  John 80
  Mary Anne 62
Duncanson, W. M. 87
Dunkin, B. F. 101
Dunlap, Ann 84
  David E. 84
Dunning, Rachel Nevarro
  Sarah 48
Dupont, Augustine Brunson
  38
  Da. Ana 26
  F. 74
  Frances 74, 116
  Henrietta 104
  Henriette 103
  Jane D. 77
  Mary Magdalene 74
  Pierre Laurent 103
Duppa, James 123
Duprat, Sarah 119
DuPre, C. 55, 97, 118
  Cornelius 26, 119
  Danl 3
Dupre, Josias James 67
DuPre, Mary E. 26
  Mary Elizabeth 123

Dupree, Thos J. Jas. 33
Dupryee, Mary Ann 68
Dupuy, John 105
Durbee, Josephene 54
Durioux, Cecile Henriette
  73
Dursse, Heloise 11
Duval, Susan 4
Dyzell, Sarah 87
Easterling, Charlotte 14
  Rebecca 10
Eaves, Sarah (Mrs.) 87
Eberhard, Emeline 109
Eberly, John 116
Eckhard, Jacob 87
Edgeworth, Emily 51
Edings, William 23
Edmonston, C. 78
Edmundston, (?) 63
Edwards, Alexander 53
  Alexander Marion 7
  Alsey 36
  Ann 42
  Ann M. 42
  Caroline Parker (Mrs.) 111
  George 43, 107
  E. H. 42
  Eliza 35
  Harrie 80
  Isaac 78, 81
  J. 28
  James F. 42, 111
  James Fisher 7
  John D. 39
  Rebecca (Mrs.) 80
  Rebecca Bee 7
  Thomas H. 35
Ehney, Mary 23
  William 23, 35
Elders, John 35
Elfe, Hanna 59
  Isaac 35
  John P. 89
  Rachel 108
Elizer, E. 13
  Eliazer 62
Elliott, Adelaide G. 44
  Bard. 118
  Benjm 93
  Charles 3
  Charlotte (Mrs.) 107
  Chas. 101
  Frances 35
  Juliet G. (Mrs.) 44

141

Elliott (cont.)
  Juliet Georgiana 35
  Maria B. 51
  Mary B. 94
  Mary C. 35
  Mary M. 39
  Phoebe 94
  Phoebe Caroline 94
  Rebecca P. 94
  William 94
Ellis, Edmund 36
  Elizabeth Capers 70
  James 25
  Mary 50
  Peggy 29
Ellison, John 104
Elmore, Catherine 23
Elstob, Elizabeth 36
Emanuel, Isaac 85
  N. 29
  Nathan 66
Emerson, Sally 101
England, Maria 76
English, Angeline 116
  Angelique 116
  Eliz. 58
  Harriet 108
  James 21
  Mary 92
Enlow, Joseph L. 120
Ervin, James 46
  Mary Elizabeth 8
Erwin, Valentine 70
Escalon, Cidalise 86
Esnard, Francoise Antoin-
    ette Carina 7
Esse, Marie Pieron de 99
Estes, Mary 57
Evans, Elizar H. 92
  George 73
  James 115
  John 100
  Josiah J. 113
  Mary (Mrs.) 23
  Rebeckah 5
  Rebekah 54
  Robert 54, 90
  Sarah 90
  Thos 106
  William 23
Eve, Esther 20
Eveleigh, Thomas 44
Everingham, John 104
  Rebecca 104

Everingtham, John 128
Ewing, Adam 45, 64, 91, 108
  Agnes Bolton 64
  Elizabeth 45
  James 64, 91
  Jane 91
  John 64
  Margaret 108
  Robert W. 91
  Robert William 64
Faber, (?) (Rev.) 9
  Charles (Rev.) 18, 24,
    84, 119, 121
  Eliz. 10
  Wm. G. 81
Fabian, John, Sr. 37
Fair, Elizabeth 88
  Richard 88
Fairchild, Alex 16
Falconer, William 126
Fanning, Ann Eliza 17
Fanse, Jeanne 50
Farrah, Bridget 87
Faupaint, Marie 40
Fayolle, Adelaide 46
Fayssoux, (?) 125
  Ann 80
  Ann Wragg 9
  Helen 9
Featherstone, Mary E. 1
Felder, Margeret 54
Fendin, Thomas 75
Fengeurs, Agatha 34
Ferguson, (?) (Mrs.) 73
  Ann 32, 60
  Anna B. 75
  B. 40
  Barkley 60
  Bartley 32
  Elizabeth 79
  Elizabeth Milner 61
  James 94, 95
  James Edward 60
  Mary O'Riely 61
  Sophia 38
  William E. 60
Fewox, Joshua 31
Fickling, Eliza 74
  Francis 41
  Henry 89
Fields, Ann 13
Finch, Joseph 116
Finley, James E. B. 4, 50
  James E. B. (Dr.) 124

Furlong, Margaret 14
Furman, Richard (Rev.) 59,
  67
  Richd. (Rev.) 18, 23,
    25, 32, 49, 50, 90
Gabeau, Elizabeth 18
  Mary-Hannah 125
  Susan 37
Gable, Caty 107
Gabriel, Mary 18
Gadsden, Benjn C. 107
  Christopher 69
  Christopher E. 110
  Christopher E. (Rev.)
    98
  Christopher Edwards 49
  Christr. E. 80
  E. A. (Mrs.) 103
  James William 2
  Jas. (Mrs.) 11
  John 7, 42, 53
  Mary Edwards 35
  P. 3, 125
  Rachel 111
Gaillard, Florida Lydia
  28
  John 28, 115
  Mary 115
  Peter, Jr. 42
  Peyre 28, 115
  Theodore 28
Galbreath, John 92
Gale, Phebe 35
Gallagher, Julia 39
  Maria 65
  Rosana 55
  S. F. (Rev.) 68
  Simon Felix (Rev.) 39,
    116
Gamble, Wm. 34
Gambrell, James 20
Gant, Thomas John 20
Gantt, Frances 65
  Thomas Jno 73
Gapper, Elvia 112
Garardeau, Emily 9
Garden, Alexander 9
  Alexander (Dr.) 53
  Alexr. 125
  Alexr. W. 78
  Eliza Gardenia 44
  Flora 6
  Harriet H. (Mrs.) 6
  Martha 122

Gardner, Harriet Hockley
  6
Gardnes, George 106
Garick, Anne 98
Garlington, Dickie 52
Gates, Anna Mary 61
  Charlotte 76
  Elisabeth 81
  John 73
  Mary Catharine 51
Gauff, Peter 102
Gaunt, Kerenhappock 37
  Zebulon 44
Geddes, Henry 114
  John 37, 128
Geffkon, Carolina 70
Gelzer, Thomas 57
Gennerick, John Frederick
  121
  Justina Louisa 121
Genoble, Margeret 95
Geoffroy, Elizabeth 70
Gerald, Zilpha 44
Germany, Jane 103
Gerreld, Bethel 44
Gettner, Lydia Ann 78
Geyer, Eliza Bampfield 76
  John S. 6
Giagnard, James S. 55
Gibbes, Ann Lewis 106
  Eliza 128
  Emma A. 106
  James L. 106
  John 45
  John Reeve 44
  John Reeves 106
  Joseph S. 106
  Lewis 35, 125
  Mary 5
  Robert 35
  Robert, Jr. 44, 106
  Robert A. 33
  Robert Reeves, Jr. 45
  Sarah 45
  Sarah Reeves 125
  William Hasell 125
  Wilmot S. 33, 44
  Wm. Hasell 68
Gibbs, Eliza 126
  William Hasell 53
Gibert, Elizabeth 71
Gignilliat, Gabriel 64
  John 117
  Margaret P. 117

Gignilliatt, Mariann
  Gendron 95
Gilbert, Barnardus M. 60
  Harriet 56
  Lucy 66
  Marie Madelene 92
Gilbreath, Charity 92
  John 92
Gilchrist, Adam 68
  Duncan 104
  Robert Budd 17
Giles, Othniel J. 122
Gill, Polly 111
Gilleron, Francoise Judeh
  Ve. 103
  Francoise Judith 103
Gilliland, Susan A. 26,
  75
Gillison, Chas. 79
Gilmer, Lucy Ann Sophia 10
Girardeau, Elizabeth Mary
  Ann 63
  John, Sr. 89
  Peter B. 17, 47, 63
Girrardeau, Peter 9
Gissendanner, Daniel 56
  John 56
Gist, John 13
Gite, Marie Jeanne 117
Giuluiany, Susanne 20
Givens, Elizabeth 70
  Philip 106
Glaise, Jane 105
Glaumont, Madelaine 72
Glaze, John 55
Gleize, Henry 41
Glisson, Sarah 47
Glover, Elizabeth
  Margaret 65
  Nancy 108
  Sanders 37, 91, 101
  Willy H. 106
Godard, Franciade M. 120
  Rene 104
Godbold, Thos. 45
Godesros, Marianne 12
Godfrey, Ann 84
  John 84
  Mary 3
  Sarah 92
Godfry, Mary 106
Good, (?) 63
  Francis 102
Goodman, Nancy 12

Goodwin, Chas 71
  Margaret 90
Gooth, Francis 102
Gordon, Eliza 67
  Elizabeth (Mrs.) 122
  James 67
  Martha 67
Gough, Catherine 18
  George William 5
  John 88
  Mary 6
  Mary Margaret 5
  Parker 59
  Roger S. 88
Goultier, Joseph 40, 100
Gourdin, Ellinor 75
Govan, Elizabeth Ann 101
Gowdey, Mary Deborah Lee
  31
Gowens, Sally 79
Gradick, Chrs. 37
Graham, Angus 94
  Jane 127
Granby, Charlotte 67
Grant, Adriana 111
  John 38, 56
  William 26, 32, 56, 104,
  127
  Wm 36
Grants, William 79
Grathan, Eliza 59
Grattan, Ann Eliza 71
  Ralph 71
Graves, Eliza. 48
  Louisa Carolina 118
  Louisa Caroline 48
  Richard 118
Gray, Aminta 109
  B. H. 6
  Jane 30
  Margaret 58
  Rebekah H. 108
  Rosannah 27
Grayson, Edward J. 25
  James 106
Greaves, Mary Ann 2
Green, Edmond 71
  Edmund 116
  Francis 68
  Harrit 89
  Jane, Jr. 55
  Jas. 55
  Margaret 79
  Martha 89

Harris (cont.)
Margaret 93
Mary 53
Sarah 89
Sarah Tucker 107
Sophia H. 55
Tucker 107
Tucker (Dr.) 15
Hart, Bella 29
Hannah 31
Jane 29
Rachel 98
Simon Moses 31
Harth, Leo 103
Sarah 103
Harvel, Sarah 57
Harvey, Elizabeth 13, 77
Frances Ann 49
Frances Anne 49
Sarah 18
Unity 21
Wm 54
Harvie, Sarah 6
Hasell, Andrew 5, 71
George Paddon Bond 5
Hatter, E. B. (Mrs.) 110
Hattier, Henry 113
Hatton, Marian 51
Hauck, (?) 17
Magdelen 16
Haupt, George 54
Haus, Anne Cecelia 41
Hawes, Ann Eliza 41
Mary 41
N. 2
Nathaniel 41
Hawie, Sarah 6
Hawkins, Ann 54
John 26
Margaret 54
Mary 26
Nathan 54
Sarah 26
Hay, Ann G. 73
Robert M. 46
Hayes, Lydia E. (Mrs.)
83
Hayne, William Edward
107
Hazel, Thomas 97
Hazelden, Ann 71
Hazlehurst, G. A. 54
Heape, Henry 40
Mary 40

Hear, James O, Jr. 78
Heath, Jno D. 91
Heazelden, Anny (Mrs.) 71
William, Sr. 71
Heckell, Catharine 122
Hector, C. J. 48
Heffernon, Mary 126
Heft, Elizabeth 122
Helegas, Philip 83
Heminger, Margt. 113
Henderson, Martha 57
Nathaniel 57
Rebekah 57
Henkle, Paul (Rev.) 112
Henlan, Adele 38
Henning, Thomas 55, 106
Hennis, David 119
Henry, Jacob 121
Heriot, Benjn A. 17
G. W. 55
Geo 118
George 55, 110
John O. 17
Maria 55
Roger 55
Will. 111
Herndon, Rachel 28
Heron, Benjamin (Capt.) 4
Elizabeth 4
Heronville, Marie Jeanne 7
Herrington, John 20
Susannah 20
Herron, John 64
Hewson, Thos. 19
Hext, Elizabeth 96
John B. 89
Lau 15
Sarah C. 15
William 96
Heyward, Ann 56, 78
Hannah Shubrick 117
Nathaniel 110, 117
William 117
Hibben, Eliza 72
Hildrup, Susannah Elizabeth
70
Hill, Eleanor 107
Whitman C. 38
Hilldrup, Susannah (Mrs.)
70
Hillgendorf, Johanna Maria
87
Hilton, William 26
Hinds, Thos 87

147

Hinson, Martha 47
Hiron, Ann 21
  John 21
Hirons, Ann 30
Hislop, Eliza 28
Hoagain, Benjn 38
Hoban, Catharine 33
Hodge, Ann 57
Hodges, Sam. 28
  Sam K. 102
Hodgkinson, Ann (Mrs.)
  53
Hodgson, John 94
Hoff, Jacob S. V. M. 1
  Jane 1
  Thomas V. M. 102
Hoffman, Elisabeth 58
Hofman, Marie Eve 70
Hogan, Alley 21
  Ann 99
Hogarth, Charlotte 1
Hogg, James 36
Holding, Jas. 116
Holland, Edwin C. 46, 47
  John 28
  Sarah 107
Holliday, Eliza 75
Hollingsworth, Ann 88
  Isaac 111
  Joseph 57
  Margaret 57
  Sarah 111
  Susannah 111
Hollinshead, William (Rev.)
  39, 56
  Wm. (Rev.) 7, 33
Holloway, Elizabeth 53
Holman, Caty 87
Holmes, Caroline 58
  Henry M. 7
  Henry P. 58
  Isaac 2
  J. E. 42
  Jane 2
  Jno 125
  John Bee 80
  John W. 58
  Margaret 104
  Mary E. 58
Hood, John 122
Hooper, Elizabeth 96
Hopkins, Ebenezer 58
Hopton, Sophia Jeanerette
  67

Horn, John 110
  Nancy 77
Hornby, E. 114
Horne, Reuben 94
Horry, Daniel 58
  Elias 30, 107
  Peter 61
Hort, Robert Smith 80
Houser, Magdelen 39
Houston, Betsy 14
  Eliza 7
  Mary A. 97
Houstoun, Harriet 97
  James E. 97
Howard, Ann 44
  Catharine 88
  Louisa 38
  Mary 126
  Richard 71
  Robert 71
  Roxanna 62
  Sarah 51
Howell, J. M. 30
  John, Jr. 16
  W. R. 16
Howren, Nimrod 59
Huaff, John C. 34
Huber, Magdelen 5
Hubert, Frances Charlotte
  56
Hudson, Elizabeth 13
Huff, Saml 23
  Samuel 120
Huger, (?) 72
  Alfred 9
  Ann Elliott 69
  Daniel E. 35, 69
Huggans, Mary 112
Huggins, Eli 16
  Nathan 25
  Robert 25
Hugher, Nancy 58
Hughes, Arthur 32, 40, 60,
  87
  Betsy 101
  Eliza S. 40
  L. E. 60
  Susannah L. 32, 60
Hughs, Arthur 60
Hume, Ann 108
  Charlotte 74
  Katherine 108
  Robert 117
Humphreys, R. W. 17

148

Martin (cont.)
  Mary Eliza 104
  N. T. 98
  Sarah A. 104
  Sarah C. 19
  Sarah Fowler (Mrs.) 104
  William 56
  William D. 98
Martindale, J. C. 11
  James C. 88
Martinet, P. C. 84
Marvin, A. 118
  Aaron 114
Mason, Hannah 5
Mathews, (?) (Mrs.) 63
  Frances 80
  George 80
  Harriet 32
  Jas. 52
  Jno Moore 107
  John K. 32
  John R. 64
  John Raven 80
  John W. 26
  John Ward 68, 80, 107
  M. A. (Mrs.) 103
  Thomas 26, 80, 118
  William, Jr. 80
  Wm. 32
Mathis, Nancy 77
Matthews, Edmond (Rev.)
  73
  George (Mrs.) 62
  Robert 79
Maxcy, Milton 70
Maxwell, Sarah-McKewn 97
May, Chas. 123
  Henry U. 87
  Marianne 69
  Susan S. 46
Mayberry, Maria Thomson
  120
Mayer, Jacob R. 45
  John G. 45
  Mary Charlotte 45
Mayrant, Ann Isabella
  44
  Frances 10
  Mary Eleonora 127
Mazyck, Alexr C. 15
  Benjamin 89
  Catharine 98
  Elizabeth Washington 59
  Mary 126

Mazyck (cont.)
  Mary Jane 89
  Paul D. 15
  Sarah 124
  Stephen 89
  William 97
M'Call, Elizabeth
  Hamilton 96
McBride, Sophia 116
McCaffrey, H. 89
McCall, Amelia H. 125
  Ann 127
  Ann D. 125
  B. 6
  Elizabeth Hamilton 125
McCalla, Thomas Harrison
  35
McCallay, (?) (Rev.) 99
McCan, Edward 124
  Jerusha 124
  Mary Ann L. 124
  Mary Ann Louisa 124
McCann, Jerusha 76
McCants, Francis 32
  Jane (Mrs.) 79
  Robert 79
  William 114
McCarthy, John 26
McCaulay, George 14
McClellan, Ann R. 86
McClellan, Susanna 86
McClesky, (?) 105
McClockin, Maryann 114
McClure, Jno, Jr. 20
McCollough, (?) (Rev.) 15
  Jane 66
McConnell, James 15
McCord, Catharine 22
  Catherine 22
McCormick, Eliza 128
  Richd. 102
  Wm 83
McCrary, Jno 87
McCraven, Mary 12
McCreary, Saml 87
  Samuel 85
McCromick, Mary 99
McCulla, Jane H. 39
McCullers, Jane 79
McCulloch, Ann 38
  William 38
McCullough, (?) (Rev.) 59
  Hans 2
  Mary 17

Mussault, Henry 113
Myers, Abram 119
  Frances Maria 55
  Jacob 110
  John J. 100
  Judy 61
  Levy 55, 83
  Levy (Dr.) 87
  Mordecai 55
  Moses 83, 110
  William 116
Neal, Stephen 87
Neilson, J. S. 105
  James S. 114, 119
Neithamar, Margaret 79
Nell, Mary 107
Nelson, Christopher 45,
    64, 121
  Elizabeth 94
  Isaac 37
  Jane 5
Nephew, James 117
Nesbitt, Eliza C. 104
Nettles, Ann 103
Neufville, Eliza 68
Newsom, Treascy 77
Newton, Anthy. 68
Nicholoson, Jas 2
Nichols, Eliza 84
  Margaret 25
Nicholson, Jas. 119
Nielson, James S. 104
Noble, Jane 21
  Mary 8
  Mary A. 32
  Rachell 57
  Sarah 7
Nolen, Elizabeth 108
Norman, Mary R. 97
  Nancy 24
Norris, James C. 96
North, Edward W. 117
  Edward W. (Dr.) 95
  Jane 2
  Jane Caroline 95
  John Laurens 88
  William 73, 79
Northrup, Samuel Bird 88
Nott, Abraham 55
Nowell, Thos S. 65
Noy, Mary Ann 76
Nusom, Eliza. 74
O Hara, Daniel 79, 126
Oakford, Mary 44

Oats, Ann 30
Obagnue, P. 84
Odingsell, Sarah 100
O'Donall, Susan 31
O'Driscol, Dens. 37
O'Driscoll, Anna Rachel 123
Oeland, John 23
Ogier, Jno M. 46
  L. 81
  Thomas 81
O'Hara, Charles 66
  Henry 66
  Rebecca 66, 78
O'Keefe, Eliza Amelia 52
Oliphant, Elizabeth 90
Oliver, John 89
  Mary 10
  Peter 5
  Prudence 121
  Sarah 10
Olman, Marie Joseph 55
  Mary Josepha 55
Oneale, Mary 90
Orelli, Eugenia 82
  Peter 82
Orr, Jno. D. 34
Osborn, Richard 96
Oswald, William 37
Osward, William 32
Otolen, Abraham 110
Owen, Betsy 40
  John 40
Owens, Wm. 5
Packer, James 79
Padget, Levicey 16
Pagan, Archibald 90
Pagett, Eliza 65
Palmer, Catherine 123
  Jesse 123
  John 115
  John, Jr. 42, 95
  Joseph 12
  Joseph, Jr. 42, 95
  Laommi 123
  Maham 42
  Mary 102
  Mary Eliza 123
  William 127
  William (Revd) 104
Panpalon, Marie 63
Paradis, Marie 4
Parker, Arthur M. 99
  Charles 126
  Edwin 126

Parker (cont.)
 Elisha 91
 Elizabeth 91
 Elizer Ann 25
 Emma 74
 Ferguson 88
 Jane Caroline 88
 Mary 48
 Mary Eveline 126
 Phins. 28
 Rachel 79
 Saml 6
 Saml O. 34
 Thomas 126
 William Henry 46
Parler, Anna 57
Parsons, James 52
Paschal, Jeremiah 58
Pate, Franky 14
Patterson, Andrew 15
 Catharine M. 108
 Hugh 110, 124
 John 77
 Nathl. T. 37
 Sarah 46
 William, Jr. 128
Patteson, Jane 66
Pattison, Hannah 12
Pawley, Mary Man 28
 Sarah B. 32
Paxton, Henry Warrell 20
Payen, Suzanna Albertine
 Jacquelina 78
Payne, John W. 43
 Polly 50
 William 67
Peace, Joseph 52
Peake, John S. 45, 108
 Michl 108
Pearce, R. 100
Pearson, Enoch 82
 Mary 63, 82
 Thomas 63
Pebarte, Richd McCormick
 104
Peele, Anne 91
 Passco 91
 Tabbitha 91
Peigne, Susannah 47
Pellissier, Louisa
 Antoinette 8
 Marie Gertrude 33
 Rosalie 93
Pelot, Charles 46

Pelot (cont.)
 Mary S. (Mrs.) 63
Pemberton, Elizabeth 115
 Isiah 115
 Sarah 115
Pennetier, Caroline 50
 Muirel (Mme.) 49
Penny, Ann 113
 John 113
Pepper, Ann S. 74
 Daniel P. 74
 Lydia C. 37
Percy, Catharine Amarinthea
 19
 Eliza Catherine 118
 Sophia 50
 William (Dr.) 98
 William (Rev.) 2, 19, 26,
  36, 45, 50, 59, 61, 73,
  76, 90, 99, 102, 118,
  124, 125
Perdreau, L. A. 123
Perdriau, Ann 120
 Jon. 120
 Samuel 92
Perone, Elizabethe
 Francoise 83
Perrin, Jane E. 21
Perronneau, Wm. 124
Perry, Daniel 25
 James 20
 Jane 108
 Joseph 46
 Matilda 53
 Peter S. 6
 Rebecca 46
 Walter H. 66
Perryclear, John 1
Peters, George 23
Petigru, Elizabeth 49
Petsch, Harriet 91
 Louise H. 58
Pettigrew, Alexander 34
 Ann 34
 Sarah 45
Peyre, Francis 110
Peyton, Ann 60
 Hy. 60
Phillips, Anne 46
 Annes 46
 Charles Christian 79
 Isaac 46
 John 46
 Philip 46

164

Smith (cont.)
  Peggy 28
  Peter 55, 76, 103
  Phillip S. 75
  Robert 22
  Roger 102
  S. 50
  S. W. 15
  Saml. Jr. 122
  Saml W. 90
  Samuel 38, 127
  Samuel, Jr. 127
  Samuel C., Jr. 104
  Sarah 50, 105, 119
  Savage 3, 65
  Sophia 69
  Stephen 69
  Thomas 9, 116
  Thomas, Sr. 65
  Thomas R. 112
  Thomas Rhett 102, 108
  Whiteford 110, 121
  William Stevens 83
  Wm., Jr. 9
Smoke, Catherine 61
Smylie, Andrew 93
Smyth, Caroline 55
  Jno 62
Snell, Adam 100
Snellgrove, Rauman 6
Snider, Anne 43
  Elisabeth 39
  Margaret 51
Snyder, Ann 91
Solomon, Hyam 107
  Israel 110
Solomons, Alexander 85
  Hester 78
  Israel 66
Somarsall, Sarah Matilda
  49
Somersall, William 96
Sommers, James D. 37
Souvorris, Rachael 90
Speer, Margaret 102
Speignerd, Rosina 128
Speissegger, Jno 98
Spence, Ann 122
  Jane 86
Spencer, Julia 116
  Maria (Mrs.) 47
Srevens, Danl. (Col.) 3
St. Clair, Jno 26
St. Gray, Priscilla 75

St. Johns, James 6
  Mary 6
St. Romes, Marie Francoise
  71
Stafford, Martha 95
Staggers, Barbara 34
Stanton, Eliza 121
  Mary 111
Stark, Robert 84
Stedman, Sarah 82
Steedler, Elizabeth 28
Steel, Tho. 127
  Thos 127
Steele, Sarah 95
Stent, Mary Colley 34
  Robert 120
Stevens, Ann 42
  Daniel 49
  J. H. 117
  James 8, 85
  Jervis Henry 13, 25, 62
  Mary-Ann 67
  Sarah 123
  Thos 1
Stewart, Daniel 101
  John 87
  Tabitha Ann 38
  W. C. 108
  Wilhelmina Amelia
    Charlotte 37
Stiles, Mary 114
  Mary W. 9
Stingley, Barbara 52
Stitles, Benjamin 9
Stock, Ann 108
  John 108
  Thomas 108, 112
Stoll, Eliza 124
  James G. 16
  Martha 112
  Susan G. 41
Stone, Eliza 22, 23
  Jno T. 14
  Margaret 128
Stoney, John 13
Stoutenmyer, Anne 53
  Jane 87
  Margeret 90
  Rosina 87
Street, Timothy 25
Strickland, Maryan 120
Strobel, Daniel 34
  Elizabeth 34

166

Thorne (cont.)
Mary 65
Thornhill, Amos 116
Thornton, Harriet 16
Joseph 46
Threadcraft, Ann
Margaret 115
Bethel 115
Thwing, Edward 96
G. W. 96
Tidyman, Hester Rose 33
Philip 33
Susan 33
Tillinghast, John, Jr.
115
Timothy, Ann 30
Tims, Hannah 89
Tiner, Anna 111
Tittle, Sarah 35
Tobias, Thomas 20
Toomer, Anthony 38
Sarah 15
Thomas P. 15
Tordes, Maria 31
Torrans, Rosella B. 110
W. H. 52
Tough, I. D. 43
Touris, Therese Margaret
22
Towers, George W. 75
Towle, Thos 64
Townsend, Daniel 124
Daniel J. 117
John 50
Jona 96
Toxier, Henriette 103
Trapier, Ben. F. 117
Hannah Shubrick 117
P. 107
W. W. 109
William W. 37, 69
Travis, Jos. 27
Joseph 49
Trent, M. E. (Mrs.) 21
Trescot, William 125
Trescott, William 22
Treville, Robert L. D. 70
Trezebant, Lewis 94, 124
Trezevant, John F. 36
Trice, William 94
Troup, Eliza 65
Trunker, Saml 41
Tschudy, John Jacob
(Rev.) 61

Tucker, Charles S. 6
Daniel 111
Elisabeth 106
Eliz. 36
Eliza 55
Eliza M. A. 17
Isaac 30
John 55, 118
John H. 17
Mary Elizabeth 111
Sarah Heriot 118
William B. 6
Tudor, T. B. 15
Tunno, Adam 60
Barbary 7
Turnbull, Eliza 116
Floride 29
James 109
Robert James 22
Turner, Danl. U. 52
David 1, 36
Turpin, Willm 121
Tutts, Aaron 116
Twele, Christopher 11
Twitty, Mary 128
Ulmer, Ann 16
Eliza 78
John 17
Mary A. 28
Paul 15
Umback, Margaret 93
Umimsetter, Maria D. 89
Upton, Sally 111
Vallaneuve, Susannah 47
Vanderhorst, Arnoldus
(Gen.) 30
Elias 30
Jane 30
John Stanyarne 30
Vandermissin, Louisa
Catherine Colleton 118
Vardell, Sarah 31
Vaughan, Lydia Ann 67
Vause, John T. 16
Veitch, Ann Goodbi 86
Henry 17
Margaret 17
William 86
Venter, Elizabeth 51
Veree, William 52
Vereen, Elizabeth 25
Verlin, Elizabeth 60
Vernon, (?) 126
Verree, Joseph 119

167

Williamson (cont.)
  Samuel 87
  Sarah 57, 73
  William 52
Willingham, Mary 8
Willis, Lina 9
  Milley 9
  Thomas 9
Wilson, Ann 79
  Dinah 125
  Eleanor 53
  Eliza 76
  Elizabeth Pettingale
    54
  Hugh 9
  Isaac M. 89
  J. 74
  Ja. 20
  James 69, 112
  Jas, Jr. 8
  John 125
  John F. 113
  John L. 37, 59
  Leighton 54
  Magdalena 33
  Maria 118
  Martha 113
  Mary 105
  Mary Ann 10
  Mary-Motte 121
  Robt 16
  Sarah 14, 49
  Sarah B. 20
Windon, Anna 21
Wingfield, Nancy 76
Winkler, Richard 57
Winn, Lettice 72
Winstanley, Moses 66
  Thomas 6, 63, 109
Winthrop, Augt. 76
  Augustus 50
  Charles 50
  Joseph 9
Wise, Elizabeth 52
Wish, Wm. 16
Wiss, Marie 91
Withers, Eleanor 124
  Francis 98
  Jane S. 28
  Jno, Jr. 70
  Mary 98
  Robert F. 98, 124
  Robt 68
  Robt. F. 42

Witherspoon, Eliza M. 36
  Moses 15
  Thomas 127
Witsell, Frederick C. 72
Witten, Eliza 41
  Peter 41
  Peter Robert 41
Witter, Jonathan 36
  Mary 2
  Sarah 36, 85
Woddrop, John 45
Wolf, Eliza Catherine 96
  Elizabeth Catharine 96
  John Frederick 54
  Margaret 54, 114
  Margaret (Mrs.) 116
Wood, Gracy 39
  James 65
  John (Rev.) 78
  Margaret 120
  Martha 77
  William 77
Woods, A. B. 47
  Jas 47
  Jos. 34
Woodward, Esther 38
Worster, Sampson 119
  Sarah 119
Wragg, Charlotte 94, 110
  Elizabeth 94, 95
  Henrietta 94, 95
  John 122
  Samuel 83, 95
  William 95
  William (Hon.) 110
Wrainch, Jane 99
Wright, Betsy 41
  Frances 73
  Judith 44
  Margaret 60
  Nathan 128
Wyat, Henrietta 2
Wyatt, Ann 45
  John R. 2
  Mary 56
  Violetta 93
  Violetta Lingard 41
Yates, (?) 63
  J. E. 24
  Samuel 24
Yeadon, William 70, 73,
    114
  Wm. 24
Young, Caroline 91

170